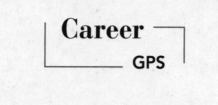

Career
GPS

Also by Ella L. J. Edmondson Bell, Ph.D.

Our Separate Ways: Black and White Women and the Struggle for Professional Identity, coauthored by Stella M. Nkomo, Ph.D.

Career
GPS

Strategies for Women
Navigating the
New Corporate
Landscape

Ella L. J. Edmondson Bell, Ph.D.

WITH LINDA VILLAROSA

Amistad
An Imprint of HarperCollins*Publishers*

A hardcover edition of this book was published in 2010 by Amistad, an imprint of HarperCollins Publishers.

FIRST AMISTAD PAPERBACK PUBLISHED 2011.

Designed by Joy O'Meara

The Library of Congress has catalogued the hardcover edition as follows:
  Bell, Ella L. J. Edmondson
  Career GPS: strategies for women navigating the new corporate landscape / Ella L. J. Edmondson Bell with Linda Villarosa.
  p. cm.
  ISBN 978-0-06-171438-2
  1. Women executives. 2. Occupational mobility. 3. Success in business. I. Villarosa, Linda. II. Title.
  HD6054.3.B45 2010
  650.1082–dc22

2009024792

ISBN 978-0-06-171439-9 (pbk.)
11 12 13 14 15 OV/RRD 10 9 8 7 6 5 4 3 2 1

Contents

Contents

Introduction

From my unique perspective as a professor at the Tuck School of Business at Dartmouth, one of the world's most renowned business schools, I am constantly amazed when I look at the confident, polished women we are sending out into the world of work. This is a new breed of corporate woman—second- and third-generation working women who are more prepared than any other generation in history. They have had access to the finest education money (or scholarships) could buy. They are well traveled and worldly, and they understand the larger global picture. Quick thinkers, they are also technically astute, smooth, and agile. I'm constantly surprised at how well they play the game, often thanks to some excellent coaching from their own mothers and fathers, who boast a wide range of business experience. Some parents walked the halls of top-tier companies, while others worked in small businesses or ran mom-and-pop companies of their own. When their daughters enter the corporate marketplace, the young women have the sense of "I belong."

This is a far cry from my own humble, shaky beginnings and those of many of my generation, who came of age in the sixties and seventies. We had little knowledge of the landscape. In fact, for me, it was so unfamiliar that it was best to look at it as foreign terrain.

Nothing in my history prepared me to enter the Ivy League elite world of education or to step into the offices of Fortune 500 companies. I was adopted into a working-class family in the South Bronx. My father had only an eighth-grade education; my mother completed only seventh grade. The business world was closed off to women in my generation. As a group, we were destined to be teachers, nurses, social workers, secretaries, and telephone operators.

In high school, one of my teachers—thank God!—looked at my record and saw that in everything but math, I got good grades. He told me, "You can go to college." That was a shocker.

I went to Mills College of Education and by my senior year was the student body president. One of the few people in my neighborhood who went to a private college, I felt extremely blessed. I was married at the very young age of twenty-one, but one of the main reasons my marriage didn't work was that I wanted to pursue a Ph.D. and my husband objected. When, newly divorced, I finally did go after the degree, my best friend's mother warned me that I was going to overeducate myself and never get married again.

In 1986 I was short-listed for a job at Yale's business school, and I was terrified. It was a chance to move into the sacred land of elite higher education, and I wondered if I really belonged. Would I get the job? If I did, would I screw up? The same year, around the same time, Whoopi Goldberg was up for an Academy Award for *The Color Purple*. Although I wanted her to win, I remember thinking that if she won the Oscar, I wouldn't get the job at Yale. My mind-set was based on scarcity: I thought in terms of limited options and opportunity. I couldn't believe the universe would bless two black women; the pie of opportunity and options didn't feel big enough. When Whoopi lost, I was sad, but I thought, *Yes! Here's my chance.*

I did get the offer to teach at Yale, and right away I called my mother. Her response was very tepid, like "Uh, oh, okay." I was disappointed that that was it. Later that evening, she called me back and told me that she had gone to the library on Fordham Road in the Bronx, because she didn't know anything about Yale and needed to understand what it was all about. The librarian had told her that Yale was an Ivy League school for rich white people, and my mother was worried that it wasn't a good place for me. "Who is going to take care of you?" she asked, clearly fearful. There were no congratulations on my accomplishment.

These days, my female students have mothers, fathers, and even grandparents who graduated from schools such as Yale. They are extraordinarily prepared; they have been preparing since kindergarten. Though these women are blessed with gifts, privileges, and opportunities I never dreamed of, they are still not ready. Despite their polish and drive, their skills, education, and confidence, there is still plenty to trip up these women in this complicated, fast-changing corporate landscape. That's why I decided to write this book.

It's because they are so prepared that they think all of the barriers have been removed and all they have to do to succeed is be competent and skilled—that discrimination is over. They think the world has changed *completely* and that women are treated just like men, people of color just like whites. Even in the era of Barack Obama, this isn't entirely true, of course. There are still biases, both in terms of attitudes toward women and people of color and in terms of discrimination found in organizations' practices and policies.

Even setting aside the residual discrimination that still exists, my students have a ways to go. Though they have the smarts, the game has changed, and they generally lack the practical, social, and emotional skills necessary in present-day companies to ascend to the highest levels.

I was recently consulting at a large, well-established family corporation and had an intense counseling session with a very bright,

well-educated, and skilled young woman. She was in the early
stages of her management career and had been with the company
for about a year and a half. She complained of being supremely
frustrated and stalled. "I work so hard, but I'm not getting promoted," she told me in tears. "I have a mentor, I attend seminars,
and I think I'm doing everything right. But nothing's happening.
I'm thinking I'll just quit."

After listening to her for a while, I asked about her social interactions. "Have you had coffee with any of the senior people in
your area?" I asked.

"No, why should I do that?" she responded. "That's a waste of
my time."

This woman's attitude is similar to that of many, many other
young women. Without realizing it, she was very focused on her
career in the narrowest sense. She put her nose to the grindstone and never looked up. She was stuck in old-school corporate
thinking.

In the new corporation—which is international, relies on technology, and has a smaller middle-management level—you have
to do so much more than work hard. (But you do have to work
very hard!) You must also show that you are socially competent,
using all of your emotional intelligence. This means developing
people and relationships. The young woman I was working with
didn't understand that. Like many others, she didn't want to do
the work to build the relationships that are necessary to move forward. She thought it was enough to do her job and go home. But
people need to know who you are and what you bring to the table.
To do that, you have to interact with people on a social level. In
fact, a high-level corporate friend once told me that early in your
career you're paid for what you do. Later you're paid for whom you
know.

Starting out, skills and performance are always 100 percent of what is required. If you're a woman or a person of color, it's probably 110 percent. You need that just to get a foot in the door. But at higher levels, those who succeed have a more subtle set of qualities. They are team players, they're top-notch communicators, and they've created an internal buzz about themselves. They care about developing other people as well as themselves because that's what leaders do. They have learned to integrate their work lives and personal lives. Without complaint (in public, at least) they are on call 24/7. These women and men have done their homework and know the company inside out; they understand where it fits in the larger industry, where it's been, and where it's going. They are flexible: they can move not only up but also laterally. And they are leaders, able to motivate, communicate, inspire, and make tough choices. These are the skills that separate those who thrive from those who merely survive.

But there's one more thing, and it's extremely hard to grasp. In order to succeed you have to bring your whole self to the table. This is especially true today. Advances in technology have created greater transparency. Everybody's watching. So the higher you ascend, the more important it is to be authentic and comfortable with yourself. The finest, most accomplished, most effective leaders don't hide who they really are. In fact, the best leaders generally have a great deal of self-awareness and have learned from the bitter and painful experiences that shaped their lives and enabled them to move ahead.

When I explain this concept to both my students and my consulting clients in corporations around the globe, I often get confused looks or blank stares. Many of them see leadership in the old pattern—the mold of the great white father. But this is an outdated paradigm, and older employees often have the most trouble with this new, more open style of leadership. The old way was to watch, listen, learn, and copy. When I started out, I patterned myself after the white male I thought I needed to be in order to fit in. Rather than being a leader, I was a follower.

I spent all my time trying to turn myself into one of the white boys. I straightened my hair, got a couple of very basic dark suits, and did what my advisor told me to do: "Don't push any buttons." My only concession was that on my lapel I wore a little African pin, an *akaba* doll, to remind me who I really was.

Finally, after not too long, I realized that I wasn't happy, wasn't fulfilled, and wasn't getting anywhere. So I took the time to redis-cover my passion and to follow it. I cut off the perm and got my natural hair back. I ditched the European, male-centric clothing and threw on some flowing outfits and bright colors. That's when I got my voice back, and that's when my career began to thrive both in research and in the classroom. The lesson I learned was that you can get in the door, but you won't be successful, particularly as a leader, unless you bring your whole self in. That's a lesson I want to teach in this book, along with encouraging you to bring passion to everything you do.

I'd also like to share another critical lesson, one that's not in most business books: the importance of being happy. This book cannot just be about how to succeed in what is a spanking new, highly competitive, hard-driving corporate world. It's also got to be about finding happiness and fulfillment. The people who are most successful in the highest levels of companies are not single-minded, seemingly psycho workaholics. They have lives—whole lives—that give them pleasure and joy.

As you read this book, I think you will find yourself in the pages that follow. I worked very hard to be inclusive. I often don't see myself in career books for women. So I made sure that this is a book for all women in various stages of their careers. I put special emphasis on the experiences and challenges of women of color. It can be difficult for any woman, but it's especially hard for those of us who are black, brown, or yellow and/or who come from humble origins. I am especially sensitive to those of you who are immigrants and/or first-generation corporate. I understand that you weren't socialized early on about the corporate world. You didn't have a father who sat at the dinner table schooling you about business issues as he talked about his day. And your mother didn't take you with her to work, where you could play "executive." With no one in your family or social circle to help you navigate the tricky corporate waters you're now swimming in, you may lack some of the common experiences that a second- or third-generation corporate woman has access to.

I also understand that if you are the first in your family to be a corporate player, everybody may be proud of you, but you have to be careful not to "brag on yourself" too much. Things happen that you can't say to anybody. You can't always tell your family when there's a success and definitely don't tell anyone when there's a failure. You are probably the one in the family—including the extended family—with the most education, status, and money, so people come to you for help and support. You become the anchor, trying to keep everyone afloat—even if you aren't ready to be that anchor because you need help yourself. It's very frustrating.

I know the stories, because I had a similar one. You may be the first in your family to move from a working-class environment to a white-collar one. Your mother, an Irish immigrant, may have cleaned houses like the ones your colleagues grew up in.

You may be from Latin America—the firstborn who had to help your mother and father by doing all the translating and maybe more. Or you're from rural Alabama, Maine, Alaska, or Arizona—the one who made it through school, while your brothers and sisters didn't and they need your help. Or this is your first job and everybody's turning to you, including your grandparents in your native country—whether it's India, Mexico, Ghana, China, or Peru. Or you used the ABC program to get to boarding school and then Harvard, while your brother barely made it through high school—or, worse, he's in prison. Or you're at the lunch table listening to your colleagues talk about the great vacations to Europe or the Caribbean they had as kids. You didn't have squat as a kid, so you become invisible in that conversation. You don't want to talk about what really happened to you; because of your class and social location, you're just too different.

Many books unintentionally leave us out. They assume that everyone had a mama or daddy before them who knew their way around the halls of corporate America. That everyone breezed through school, popped into Harvard or Yale, and grabbed an MBA along the way. Then entered the corporation—and oh my God, what's this? A ceiling . . . made of glass?

Whether you were raised with a silver spoon stuck firmly between your teeth or all you had was a used plastic fork or one splintered chopstick, I will not leave you out. This book is for you.

If you're just starting out or returning to the workplace after having a baby, raising a family, or taking care of parents, you'll see yourself here. If you're stuck and would like to move up—or out—you'll find advice, support, and encouragement. If you're bumping up against a glass ceiling or banging your head against a concrete one, you will see yourself in the stories of the many amazing women included throughout the pages.

I've spent years developing the ideas in this book and tracking down information that has helped me learn and move ahead in my own life. I also tapped the knowledge of many of my friends, colleagues, associates, former students, and people I admire, both as experts and because of their personal experiences and wisdom. My goal is to offer a book for every one of you who wants to find your way in the newly reshaped and reinvented corporate geography.

You'll notice that, at the end of this book, I've included a "Memorandum to the Executive Team." I added this section to make it clear that, though I offer plenty of strategies for working women, it is not only up to individual women to "fix themselves." Rather, corporations must engage in serious change efforts to both retain and advance their women. The playing field is not level, and it's way beyond time for companies to get their houses in order.

I would be remiss if I didn't address the current economic situation. When I started this book, land was plentiful and the skies were blue, or so we thought. As I finished it, there was a whole new economic landscape. Banks are failing, corporations are restructuring if not going out of business altogether, and many, many people at every level are losing their jobs. Some of you who were racing up the ladder may now be struggling to hang on or have fallen off.

In this climate, the advice on the pages that follow is not just important; it's critical. If your company is in the midst of restructuring and layoffs, I can't give you the blueprint that will help you dodge the pink slip. But if you've used the ideas offered in *Career GPS*, you will land on your feet. First and foremost, those who are spared the corporate ax are the high performers whose reviews provide a clear record of their accomplishments and whose responsibilities, assignments, and goals are in line with the bigger vision of the company.

In our modern corporations, you must also have the ability to transcend corporate borders and move between different areas of the company. Having skills and competencies that are both broad and deep and being able to juggle multiple responsibilities or do more than one job all increase your value. At best you have international experience; at the least you have a grasp of the global marketplace. You must be a team player and, even better, be able to lead a team. Your brand should be rock-solid and the buzz about you steady. You have to have strong relationships at all levels, both formal and informal. Ideally, you have a mentor and a sponsor, so when the hard decisions are made behind closed doors, there's someone who can vouch for you. And if, God forbid, you are laid off, you have a twenty-first-century resume ready, and you know how to use technology to aid your job search and work your network to help you find your next position. I go into these areas and more in depth, and offer you lots of role models to help you shore up your career and confidence for as long as the waters remain rough.

Even if you feel insecure and unsure about what the future holds for you, I ask you to stand tall. Now more than ever is the time to draw upon your unshakeable faith and the belief that this too shall pass. You *will* have the career and the life you have dreamed of and that you deserve. It's your time. Companies need women like you to provide the leadership that is required to chart a new course.

Allow me to guide you. Let this book be your road map, your compass, your career GPS. Now put on your walking shoes and let's go.

Ella L. J. Edmondson Bell, Ph.D.

Career
GPS

Chapter 1

Discovering and Embracing All of Who You Are

Success starts internally, and most successful people know that. Companies are looking for effective leaders, and the first tenet of effective leadership is self-awareness. That means it's critically important to know who you are and to be comfortable in your own skin.

In the demanding new corporate reality, understanding yourself is key. Self-knowledge makes you more genuine, authentic, and confident—three traits you need to make smart career choices and manage all of your corporate responsibilities. It's best to know yourself before you get in the game, but understand that self-awareness grows throughout the process. Even after you leave your job, you need to understand how to develop yourself as you move to the next stages of your life and career.

In this chapter I'll explain the extreme importance of knowing yourself fully. I'll also ask you to do two exercises. One will help you examine the good, the bad, and the ugly parts of your life and begin the process of healing and letting go. The other allows you to look at your whole life and reflect on your journey thus far. Each of these will help you establish a more authentic, confident, and grounded *you*.

Being Yourself—Whoever You Are

I met Sukshma Rajagopalan when she took part in one of my leader-ship development workshops. I was impressed with her authenticity, her ability to bring her whole self with her wherever she goes. Origi-nally from India, she came to the United States at age twenty on a Rotary scholarship. She is a mature, grounded young woman who has created a comfortable life here while holding on to the parts of her culture that are important to her.

Sukshma is also the rare woman who's found career success in the information technology arena, which is essentially still a man's world. With an MBA from the University of Houston, she started as PepsiCo's business solutions manager for the IT group in 2005 and was promoted to senior manager two years later. Not long ago, she was promoted again, to group manager. I asked her to discuss how she integrates her cultural beliefs and values into her work environment.

————

Though I had been raised and educated in India, when I first came to America I didn't feel different. I didn't think of myself as an Indian or as a woman; I was just me. When I dressed in ethnic clothes, people looked but they didn't stare. Generally, they'd say things like "I love what you're wearing" or "Your silk is so beautiful."

Though I was raised with a strong sense of Indian culture, now, years later, I've become very American—as my mom tells me at least thirty times a day. But not totally; my culture is integrated into the life I have here in Texas. My husband, my parents, and I do Indian ceremonies at home, and we wear traditional dress on special occasions or when we go out.

At work, I have pictures of my family all over my cubicle and people often stop and admire them. My spirituality is important to me, so I also have a painting of my God, Krishna. Some people walk by and wonder out loud if it's a picture of a friend or relative. Others look but don't know if they can ask. If I see them looking, I don't shy away from talking about it. It's a good conversation point and gives people an opportunity to know who I am and what I'm about. We spend so much time talking about work all day that sometimes it's nice just to talk about who you are.

THE IMPORTANCE OF KNOWING YOURSELF

Why is self-awareness critical? Your skills, talent, knowledge, personality, and strengths are your best assets as a professional woman, a manager, and a leader. Let me be more specific.

Self-knowledge builds confidence. Now, I didn't say "boosts ego," and I definitely don't mean "makes you cocky." We all know people who act supremely sure of themselves. They seem full of confidence, but I bet they are trying to hide some deep insecurities or fears. What confidence is *not* is acting like you're the hottest thing out there because you've got an MBA from a top-ten school. Behaving like everything's "all about me." That's not what I mean by confidence; any perceptive person can see right through someone like that.

Part of knowing yourself is being sure of you. But another part is understanding when your ego is out of control and knowing how to pull yourself back.

Self-awareness is one cornerstone of effective leadership. Leadership is one of the qualities companies look for aggressively, but you can't develop anyone else unless you've developed yourself. And this means making the time to do the "me" work. Being an effective leader requires integrity, courage, and vision. People have to be able to trust their leaders, so you need to be able to talk the talk *and* walk the walk. A good leader knows "the buck stops here." Other people see that she understands what's important, what's at stake. She knows when to take risks, when to pull back, and how to sort through choices and make tough decisions.

Leadership isn't about the "big me." Self-aware leaders are able to see the larger picture, the context and purpose. They actively listen and don't put themselves ahead of others. They create a culture where others can flourish and be the best that they can be.

Without the grounding and the kind of direction that comes from having done the work that leads to self-knowledge, you're like a handkerchief in the wind. When a conflict or difficult issue comes up, you're unsure, your story shifts, your direction changes. That's not effective leadership. In order to be a person others look up to, trust, and are willing to follow, you must be sure of who you are and what you think. Self-examination is the way to get there.

Being sure of who you are and what you want allows you to make sound career decisions. In today's world, there are so many choices, and many of these options have only recently opened to women. So if you're at the beginning of your career—or at a crossroads—having a better sense of who you are and what you want can help you push away things that are not really important and urge you to go after the things that are really in your heart. (I'll help you do more of this work in Chapter 2.)

For instance, if you're signing up for a very high-level job at an international company, you need to ask yourself a few questions: What are you willing to give up to work around the clock? How far are you willing to stretch? Would you be willing to move to a new city, state, or even country for the right job? Living abroad might be a brilliant career move, but is it right for you—for the person you really are, the family you have? Will you be too far from an ailing parent? Do you want your children to go to an international school?

Knowing, accepting, and liking who you are encourages others to do the same. Being authentic and genuine makes you attractive as a new hire, liked and respected as a colleague, and effective as a leader. Unlike in the past, when conformity was more the norm, today individuality is encouraged and prized.

Finding Your Own Special "Medicine"

LaDonna Harris, president and founder of Americans for Indian Opportunity, is a Native American activist and visionary. She is one of the wisest, most powerful, and most successful leaders I have ever met. Well regarded in corporate circles, she sits on the advisory boards and councils of several Fortune 500 companies, which are eager to tap into her insights and wisdom on diversity and leadership. I asked her to explain how she discovered what she calls her own "medicine" and share her vision for cultivating the gifts of others.

———————

I was raised by my Comanche grandparents, and the basic philosophy of our social structure, and that of many North American tribes, is that every person has value—something to contribute to the whole. We think of it as your own special "medicine."

I was fortunate to recognize my medicine at a young age, which made a huge difference in my life. As a child I was dyslexic, but I didn't know it at the time. I thought I was stupid, that I couldn't read or spell. I had very low self-esteem and spent a lot of time studying people. I became almost nonverbal, a stoic Indian girl.

But my grandmother saw something more in me; she saw that I was going to be a leader. With her, I showed a great interest in our Comanche culture. I was curious and always asking questions. She helped me grow and develop by exposing me to new experiences and giving me responsibilities greater than those of most children my age. I spent a lot of time with elders and attended meetings and ceremonies; I responded by learning and observing and growing stronger and more confident.

I believe my special medicine is recognizing the gifts that others have to offer. To me, this means recognizing the value in each person, acknowledging it to them, and making them feel good about their contribution. This is what leadership is.

If you understand that everyone has something to offer—their medicine—you'll be able to bring out the best in each person. My grandmother taught me to watch and observe in order to figure out the gifts other people have to offer. Once you recognize someone's medicine, you nurture it and help that person grow, like my grandmother did for me. Leadership is getting people to respond by nurturing their gifts and making them feel good about whatever they have to contribute. It means never leaving anyone behind, because each individual contributes to the success of the whole.

Understanding your wants and needs helps you say no when necessary. More than ever, jobs are very demanding. At the highest levels, you'll be expected to be present just about 24/7 while keeping everything else in your life managed. With so much out there and so much to do once you're in place, knowing your limits—just how far you can stretch before you break—is an important skill.

For women, this is essential. We tend to try to make everybody else happy, and we give up what's important to us for the success of the organization, for the people we work with, and for the folks we love. Many of us do that because we think that's how to get ahead and, even more, that's how to be liked and loved.

But if you know yourself, it'll be easier to determine exactly what you need to tolerate in order to be successful—and what you don't. You'll be sure to put yourself into the equation at the forefront, not as an afterthought. Self-awareness helps you hear and then listen to your voice within. Vision, good leadership, success, and joy don't come from someone who's only about go-go-go, do-do-do. You have to take time to close your eyes, exhale, and get in touch with your wise inner self to be effective.

ALL OF YOU: THE GOOD, THE BAD, AND THE UGLY

No one, even the best of us, is all good. It's important to know, understand, and accept all of who you are—the good, the bad, and the ugly. Cultivating that kind of self-awareness helps you determine your growth edges, the areas where you may need to develop and stretch. I don't like to describe these areas as weaknesses. A weakness sounds like a fatal flaw, something that makes you feel vulnerable or that is permanent and can't be fixed.

Instead, we all have developmental needs. Some are based on our prior experiences and the pain that we've had on our life journeys. They can be physical, emotional, or spiritual. Others are cognitive or technical, signaling that we need more education, instruction, or training. For many women particularly, developmental needs—especially in the corporate area—come from not having role models, mentors, or coaches or not being exposed to corporate environments. Developmental learning is a lifelong process, and those who are willing to grow and stretch will discover a rich, more exciting, and complex person inside. Or as LaDonna Harris would say, "It makes our medicine stronger."

Let me help you understand what I mean by the good, the bad, and the ugly. *The good* encompasses the parts of ourselves that we love, adore, and embrace. These are the natural gifts and treasures that you're aware of and proud of. You've probably received positive reinforcement your whole life for being a good singer, great at math, an excellent writer, or a wonderful storyteller. Your parents, teachers, neighbors, professors, and pastor have all given you positive reinforcement for these skills and traits, so it's easy to stay in the good.

Like the good, you're probably also aware of *the bad*, those parts that need work. Maybe you've got a bad temper, can't manage money, or need to exercise more. Think of these as the characteristics, traits, and behaviors that don't work for you. It's the New Year's resolution wish list: "I'm going to speak up more, lose ten pounds, learn Spanish, and take a course to beef up my tech skills." Also like the good, the bad gets reinforced in us, too— often by the same people who reinforce the good. The boundaries between the bad and the good are often loose. Most of us are conscious of our bad traits and are willing to try to make our bad characteristics good ones. Something good can become bad; something bad can become good.

The ugly is a little different. These are the parts that are generally hidden, especially from ourselves. Other people can often see them, but not always. The ugly comes from the events, experiences, and people in our lives that trigger deep shame. We don't talk about these parts we see as ugly; it's hard for us to own them. They lie deep, and because we generally aren't aware of them, they can unconsciously influence our thoughts, feelings, and actions. The ugly parts are like demons that are always with you.

They might not ever go away, but to be successful—and happy—you have to learn to dance with them. In other words, it's not about eradicating these parts; the key is to recognize that these hard, painful experiences in our lives gave us certain gifts.

Let me give you an example. I know women who grew up without a father and then went into the workplace seeking a daddy. A woman in this situation can grow too dependent on her manager or try to take care of him or protect him. Or they cross the boundary by allowing their male managers to be verbally abusive. Sometimes they don't know how to let go and move on. The male supervisor becomes the ultimate authority, causing them to squelch their own desires and lose their voices. They can't recognize what is going on, because they can't connect the dots between the loss of their father and the dependent relationship they've created with their boss. They're caught up in a behavior they can't change, because they don't recognize the psychological root.

I have my own demons that I've learned to dance with. Sometimes I hear mine talking to me; I know it's not me speaking; it's my demon, my dragon. Because my past triggers feelings of abandonment, betrayal, and anger, I have to force myself not to listen.

I was adopted, which is one of the sources of my demons. Of course, I've worked on myself, been to therapy, and done my research. I know that the parents who raised me loved me and that my biological mother and father loved me. But sometimes, especially when I'm tired or stressed, I look up and feel a big hole in my heart. I question my worthiness: *My mother gave me away as a kid; what does that say about me?* I get consumed by the orphan archetype, and I play the victim.

What I know about myself is that I have a constant need to prove that I am worthy. I pick environments that are very competitive, then drive myself to achieve. I don't listen to my body, I ignore my inner voice, and I burn myself out—all to prove that I'm

as good as everybody else. This is one demon I continually dance
with.

I have a Ph.D. from a top school, but the first time my graduate advisor told me I was smart, I was shocked. Secretly I thought
I wasn't good enough to be in that elite environment and that I
was just sneaking through. I questioned my worthiness. This is
another one of my dragons.

What's your demon? Everybody's got one, if not more than
one. There's no escaping the pain. People lose loved ones, parents divorce, children are abused, people you love are addicted,
kids are born into disadvantaged environments. The solution is
to learn when your demon is in action. If you can't manage it,
dance with it, you'll never consistently be your best self at work—
or anywhere else. At worst, you'll feel dysfunctional and even self-
destructive. Dancing is the process of reframing the ugly, learning
to forgive, and having compassion for yourself and all that you've
been through.

Learn to embrace all of who you are—the good, the bad, and
the ugly. The first step is to find a good support system of people
who care about you, love you, and will be there for you. Next,
examine your good aspects. Polish and perfect the things you
do well. Look for assignments and challenges that showcase your
good parts, and let yourself shine.

As far as the bad parts, you can work on these, so get a plan.
Take a public-speaking class. Decide you're going to be more
sociable—wear that red dress to the holiday party! Learn to swim,
get serious about losing weight, find a mentor or coach, or take a
course and learn an advanced computer program.

The ugly is more complex. To understand the ugly, you need to
be still and reflective in order to examine past events in your life
and connect the dots in your life story. The ugly requires you to
look for unique growth opportunities. That doesn't mean hanging

out with your girlfriends moaning and groaning. You have to do the work. You can gain insight into those parts of yourself through meditation, journaling, and other ways of quiet reflection. When it's too hard and painful or overwhelming, get help from a counselor, therapist, or pastor.

Let's do a little work so you can begin to tap into your self-knowledge. I'm going to ask you to look back to figure out how you got to where you are right now. Life is a continuing journey, not just a snapshot. So, if you're going to do the work around who you are, you have to take the time to understand the sum of the journey. You don't just drop into the leadership chair and start being a leader at that moment. How you lead, manage, and interact with people is based on your cumulative life, starting at birth and moving to where you are now.

The exercises I'm going to ask you to do can be very emotional. One hundred percent of the time I've used them in groups, several people—including hard-core, tough-as-nails male executives—have ended up in tears. That's okay. Tears are healing, a sign of release. Don't shy away from these feelings; they will help you become a more authentic, confident, skilled, and grounded leader. Just keep a box of tissues nearby.

Meeting Your Eight-Year-Old

HOW IT WORKS

This is a two-part exercise. First, you'll watch the movie *The Kid*, an enlightening Disney movie about what happens when an executive comes face-to-face with his much younger self. Then you'll write a letter. The goal is to know and understand yourself better and more deeply. You'll need about three hours.

WHAT YOU NEED

The Kid, from your video store or Netflix

Paper and crayons (make sure that you have your favorite color—the one you used to death on every picture in your coloring book)

HOW THIS EXERCISE WILL AFFECT YOUR WORK LIFE

The point of this exercise is to begin to connect the dots to the past and take a good look at what we've carried with us—the good, the bad, and the ugly—as adults. It's also a way to begin healing and letting go of what's no longer useful in our lives.

The wounds, pains, scars, and fears that often get in our way as adults—what some people like to call baggage—are often connected to our past, our girlhood. A number of researchers, most notably Dr. Carol Gilligan, have studied the development of girls. The preteen years are the time when girls are the most confident and self-assured. They have strong voices and know how to use them. This is a time when girls aren't all caught up with society's norms. Somehow around age thirteen, as girls get older, that confidence begins to erode and their voices begin to diminish. Connecting to that eight- or ten-year-old, particularly for women, gives us access to our early voices, our early passions, our interests, and our curiosity . . . before we were trying to be perfect in a society that often skews how young girls are supposed to behave, feel, and look.

The Kid is a typical Disney fantasy, but it has some value in helping us understand how the pains, complexities, and difficult segments of our early lives impact us as adults. Russ Duritz, played by Bruce Willis, is an arrogant, obnoxious, rich image consultant. A single, successful workaholic, he seems like he has it all. He's highly successful but emotionally stunted. When Russ is about to turn forty, dumpy, awkward

Rusty appears in his life—Russ's eight-year-old self. Russ hates the boy—the stammer, the twitch, the extra fifteen pounds. And Rusty hates Russ, too, seeing Russ as a "loser": he doesn't have a dog, he doesn't fly an airplane, and he's not married.

Take some time on a Sunday afternoon or on a rainy evening, pour a glass of wine or make a cup of tea, and watch this movie. As you watch, think how you would feel if an eight-year-old you suddenly appeared on your doorstep at this stage in your life. What do you think she'd say to you? What would you say to her? How would you connect to her? Would you be happy to see her? Would you greet her with loving arms or would you keep her at bay? What memories would she conjure in your mind?

After the movie, think back to when you were eight years old. Who was that little girl? Get a clear image in your head of what you looked like. Were you tall or short? What was your hair like? What was your favorite piece of clothing? What were your favorite activities? Foods? Books? Who were your heroes and sheroes?

Still thinking about that girl, sit down and write a letter from your eight-year-old self to the woman you are now. What would the eight-year old you say about how you are living your life today? Think like an eight-year-old and write like one, too. Please be sure to write with crayons, because eight-year-olds back then didn't use computers. Keep it simple. Limit yourself to one page. Print, because it slows down your thinking process. If you spoke or wrote in a language other than English when you were younger, then write in the language of your childhood. Talk about your life and the adult you've become.

After you're finished, take some time to read over what you've written and reflect on it. Let it into your heart, not just your brain. Examine the feelings that emerge from your gut and your heart. What stands out to you about your eight-year-old self? What really got you excited when you were a kid? What things were you afraid of? Were there things that hurt you?

If you have a journal, now's a good time to pull it out and jot down your thoughts, your feelings, and some of the answers to those questions. Be honest with yourself. Don't forget to be celebratory: look at how much you've grown, how much you've learned. Observe the woman you've become and feel good about her. Give that little girl a big hug. Look her in the eye and tell her that everybody and everything's going to be just fine in her life. Keep her in your heart. Remember that you can go back and love her, celebrate her, and play with her anytime.

Creating Your Life Line

HOW IT WORKS

Earlier, I asked you to connect yourself in the present to your eight-year-old self in the past. In this exercise, you'll connect more dots, but this time we'll look at your cumulative experience by creating a time line of your life. You should plan on spending an hour.

WHAT YOU NEED

A large sheet of butcher paper or newsprint, or several sheets of paper taped together

Pens, crayons, markers, or colored pencils to write and draw with

HOW THIS EXERCISE WILL AFFECT YOUR WORK LIFE

As we close out this chapter, I'd like you to look at your whole life using the lifeline exercise, which I learned in graduate school. It will allow you to reflect on your whole life journey so you can gain the self-knowledge that makes you more genuine, authentic, and confident. As with the exercise involving your eight-year-old self, there are no right or wrong ways to do this. You do it the way it works for you. My only suggestion is that you make some "me" time, so that you can be candid with yourself and use it as an opportunity to learn about you. You don't have to do this alone; you might want to do it with a friend or even several, so that you can share your journeys. Make a tea out of it.

On a large sheet of paper, organize the highlights of your life from childhood to present into a time line of *you*. Include everything you can remember—the place where you were born, significant people, places, and events of your life—on this continuous line. Think of it as an intimate, personal resume. This isn't a just-the-facts document; I'd also like you to note where you showed courage, risk, determination, humility, heart, vision, passion, faith, and perseverance. Part of knowing who you are is identifying your jewels, the treasures of your life. But the other part is not shrinking away from the times you messed up and freaked out—the moments you'd like to forget but shouldn't. Ultimately, it's the bad times that help you appreciate the good ones. The worst of times create the greatest opportunities to grow.

Also pay close attention to what author Alicia Britt Chole calls the "hidden years," those periods when there were no major changes or upheavals. These fallow times, when it feels like you're waiting for something to happen, are also important. They allow us to grow and stretch in preparation for opportunities and desires that we've been seeking.

As you draw your lifeline, think big. Don't try to put it on a little sheet of paper. Spread out on the floor, like in kindergarten playtime, to create your life. This is your masterpiece. You can draw in pictures and symbols if you wish. Take as long as you need to create your life journey "map."

Once you finish, take some time to reflect. Look over your cumulative life. What does it say about you? What are the blessings in your life? What was going on while you were growing up? Given the valleys and lows in life, what do you learn about your strengths? Is there a theme—something that keeps coming up? Maybe there's more than one.

Knowing Yourself: The Essentials

- *Know who you are and make sure you're comfortable in your own skin. It will help you be a strong, effective leader.*
- *Be genuine, authentic, and confident. These are the traits that will help you make smart career choices and to manage your work responsibilities.*
- *Keep your ego in check. Leadership isn't about the "big me."*
- *Cultivate others. Observe and uncover the gifts that other people possess. It will show that you're a good leader, colleague, and person.*
- *Be able to say no. It's important to know your limits and to understand how far you can stretch before you break.*
- *Explore your whole self—the good, the bad, and the ugly. Don't shy away from the parts of yourself you don't like. Examining them offers opportunities to grow.*

What's Next?

In this chapter we examined who you are—the good, the bad, and the ugly—and worked on ways to move to a deeper level of self-knowledge that will help you be a more authentic leader at work. In the next chapter, you will take your personal insights and use them to help you select and shape a job—and a career—that's right for you.

Chapter 2

Choosing the Career Path That's Right for You

I n the past, getting in the corporate door was extremely tough for us. But even given the economic ups and downs, now is a very different time: The doors are much more open for women who have the right skills, education, and attitude. But you have to be ready.

Perhaps the biggest challenge for women is selecting the right path. Not that you're going to stay on any one path over the course of your career. If you're like most people, you're likely to change career paths, perhaps more than once. But as you begin your journey or take a turn, it's best to know what you're in for before you pursue or accept any kind of position.

A few years ago one of my students learned that lesson the hard way. She got a plum job—with an astronomical salary—at one of the most elite financial houses in the world. This was a highly sought-after, extremely competitive sales position that every student wanted. And this woman deserved the big job: she was a good student who had worked hard and done her homework.

Though I was proud of her and excited about her wonderful opportunity, part of me was also worried. Was she prepared for an "extreme" job, with its crazy hours and aggressively competitive atmosphere? She might feel isolated working in a high-testosterone, overcaffeinated atmosphere; was she ready for that? Although she had the right skill set, I wasn't sure if it was the right fit. I wanted to talk to her about what she should expect and what was expected of her, and discuss what kind of life she was going to have. I also wanted to suggest ways to create balance and explain the importance of being mentored and building supportive networks both inside the company and especially outside of it. However, this young woman was so swept up in the excitement of her new challenge that she wasn't able to hear my warnings or advice.

I saw her a year later, and she was a mess. She was so stressed out that she had lost some of her hair and gained lots of weight. As she described her job, I noticed that her eye was twitching. By the end of the year she had left the job, and now she works for a nonprofit organization.

Though I was sad that it didn't work out for her, I wasn't shocked. Without a clear strategy or anyone to support and help her, the odds were stacked against her. Plus it was the wrong culture for her personality, her temperament, and her work style. That's just the reality.

The lesson here? When thinking about a job and a career path, the goal is to be mindful. That means being as intentional as you can about who you are, what you want to do, what you want to be, and where you want to work. This chapter will help you do that. I've outlined the three basic career paths and offered first-person stories of women who chose them. I also offer advice, strategies, and exercises to help you figure out which kind of job is right for you.

CHOOSING A CAREER PATH

Experts have identified three career paths in the new corporate marketplace. Structure and hierarchies, of course, differ from industry to industry, company to company. But these are the paths where the women I work with are on or aspire to be on.

Good Corporate Citizen

In the old days, this job would be called "upper midlevel management." But I prefer to think of this career path as the "good corporate citizen." This level is the sweet spot on the organizational hierarchy. They are potential candidates for the executive track but aren't there yet. Some of them don't want to be. You will find these individuals in every industry. And there are a lot more of these positions than there are slots on the executive team. They have job titles such as general manager or vice president. At banks, they're called principals and managing directors.

People seek out good corporate citizens. They maintain unbelievable networks both within the company and outside the company, inside the industry and outside the industry. They are probably also active in noncompany professional networks.

Their relationships are very important, but they've also done the work. They have a deep knowledge of the business; they're highly valued and respected. They often focus on the client and have core revenue-generating relationships. These folks are highly sought after. They're always getting calls from headhunters.

Though this isn't the executive suite, these aren't Mickey Mouse positions. Good corporate citizens can be well compensated—often six figures—and enjoy nice bonuses, retirement packages, and other perks. Still, you have to work your tail off to be in this bracket. You have to pay your dues and have good standing in the company. Some good corporate citizens may have been passed over for executive slots, but for many, moving higher wasn't on their wish list. Many women have broken through the glass ceiling and gotten to this level. If I were entering a company, good corporate citizen would be my personal aspiration. Moving higher would take too much out of me, and there are too many other things I want to do with my life.

Some of you may have your eye on an executive slot, so being a good corporate citizen feels like a stepping-stone to a better gig. And that's true for some. But let's be clear: there's only so much room at the top. Even though we're in the process of rapid change and there are more and more open chairs at the table for women and people of color, the number of upper-level positions remains small and turnover is slow. Think of it this way: King Arthur only had so many knights around his round table, and there were no knightesses! Also, life can get in the way of your plans, and your career path may change. Depending on what's going on outside work, particularly around family issues, being a good corporate citizen may be plenty of job for you.

Corporate Citizenship: Balanced and Fulfilled

Not long ago, a bright young woman attended my leadership program. I was impressed that she has managed to have it all—a job she loves, a beautiful toddler, and a fulfilling relationship. But she's also made a trade-off. The marketing director for a Fortune 500 company, she's a good corporate citizen who has pared down her ambitions in order to spend more time with her family.

————————

You really do have to choose. I love my job, and I work really hard all day. I manage several people and spend much of the day in meetings from the second I walk in, at 8:30 a.m., until I leave, at around 6:00. But when I'm finished with what is generally a very energizing, fulfilling day, I'm ready to go home.

I don't want to be in the office at all hours like I used to be. I can't attend work-related social events every night. I don't want to be at home multitasking all night long. I want to be with my husband and my daughter, and I want to give my child my undivided attention while she's awake. After she's asleep, I spend at least two more hours answering emails, writing presentations, or fleshing out a strategy. For me, that's enough.

At this point, I'd like to get promoted to vice president. That's my goal; that's what I'm aiming for. But I also want to have more children, so that means I have to work both harder and smarter. Before, I wanted to take on the world, acquire, acquire, acquire. Now I do fewer things but do them really well. I'm trying not to get pulled in a million different directions. I'm more focused, more strategic, and smarter about delegating and prioritizing all the things I have to do.

After I make VP, do I want to be a senior VP? To be honest, I'm not sure. I see how those people who are in the executive suite really live, and I don't think it's right for me. I'm not looking for anything extreme. Family is what's most important to me now.

Executive Suite

The executive suite is where the high-powered positions are, what people think of as the glamour jobs. But they are far from glamorous. They require long hours, typically sixty to eighty per week. They are directors, the chairperson of the board, the CEO, the director of HR, the CFO, the COO, the president of marketing, and senior and executive VPs. These executives are the key decision makers. You read about them in *Fortune*; sometimes they're on the cover. They make large sums of money and are rewarded with lots of perks and other goodies. They are recognized as innovators and tough decision makers, and they are brought in to transform the organization.

These leaders bring a wealth of talent and skills to the company. Many of them have been educated at some of the most elite business schools in this country or in other parts of the world. They are often very charismatic, high-touch extroverts. Others, though, are introverted, soft-spoken, and reflective. Relationships, savvy, wisdom, and work background are all very important.

The executive suite is a place to make a difference, to leave your mark. Executives at this level often transform some part of the company where they work or sometimes turn the whole company around. They're the stars, and their star grows bigger with each accomplishment.

The executive suite is very clubby, both inside and outside the company. To succeed, you must live a corporate lifestyle where personal and professional lives merge, which means working long hours, bringing work home, traveling for your job, and creating informal work relationships that are maintained outside the company. These executives often live in the same communities, go to the same churches, belong to the same clubs. You travel with your colleagues; you socialize with them. You know about each other's lives and share experiences. The workplace is your social center. Because so many companies are global, you have to be comfortable with people who are different, both within the United States and internationally.

With all that travel, the long hours, and the socializing, if you have children, you probably have lots of hired help; perhaps your husband even stays home with them.

At this level, you can't neglect your health. The best of the executives in the corporate suite take good care of themselves. You can't have a sick or unhealthy-looking CEO. So they're trim and fit—thanks to wonderful access to medical resources. They also tend to have families and children who support their spiritual and emotional needs.

There are downsides to the corporate suite. Shelf life is short. These high-level executives generally don't stay at a company longer than five years. In that time, they've taken the company as high as they can—or they've taken as much as they can of the hours and stress. Many burn out. Or they've come into the job with a tight set of goals, and once those are accomplished, their work is finished. They move on to new challenges, often to another company, sometimes in a different industry or even in a different sector.

If you really want that executive suite, but you look around and think it's hopeless that you'll ever become a CEO, keep in mind that though there are only five hundred Fortune 500 companies, there are many, *many* smaller corporations, not to mention start-ups. So if you can't find a high-level place in your company, there's still a whole constellation of other companies where you can drop your handbag and kick off your heels in the executive suite. For those of you who are really daring, you can start a company of your own.

The Executive Suite: Life Is Sweet

Deborah Elam is vice president and chief diversity officer at GE in Fairfield, Connecticut, and a wonderful example of a woman who has learned how to keep her life in balance. She landed in the executive suite about three years ago, after starting at GE twenty-two years ago while still a graduate student at Southern University in Baton Rouge. Deb is the company's first African American female corporate officer. In the organizational hierarchy, her spot is just two levels below the CEO.

Along with the big job, which includes lots of travel, Deb has a husband and two daughters and is involved in a number of community activities. She works hard and likes what she does, and manages to keep everything—and everyone—together by being highly organized and attentive to details. With a smile.

———————

I really love my job. I love the impact that I have. I love the interface with the most senior levels, and especially enjoy mentoring, motivating, and inspiring people. I'm also proud of my company. My job is to attract, develop, and retain the best talent globally, and to make sure we have a workforce that reflects the places where we work and live and do business in terms of diversity. I'm passionate about that goal and devoted to it.

I also have some qualities that make me good at what I do and also good at interfacing with people at all levels, including at the top. I'd say that I have great interpersonal skills, and I'm good at building and leveraging relationships. I also have the ability to deliver above expectations. I get things done. I try to be politically savvy. I've worked hard to understand the tea leaves, to read the signs and connect the dots. Everybody has a different style. Some people yell and pound their fist on the table to make things happen. That's not me. I try to work a crowd behind the scenes to get things done.

But I also understand that with my job comes a hectic schedule. I travel often and around the globe. I'm going to Philadelphia this week, next week Prague, then Munich. To manage it all, I get up at 4:30 a.m. to send emails and do phone calls to Europe or Asia. I have an exercise room at home, so in the mornings I try to work out for about a half hour. My thirteen-year-old gets up at 5:20, my eleven-year-old daughter at 5:45, so I push them along. We get dressed, I watch the news, and I might peek at my email until I leave around 7:00 a.m.

My husband works outside Connecticut, so he's gone Monday through Friday. I have a child care provider who gets the girls to school, picks them up, and drives them around to activities until I leave the office, around 6:30 p.m.

The only way I can handle all this—or how any successful woman can manage a full life—is by being very organized. Superorganized. Anal. I'm a list person, so that helps. But if anything were to happen to my BlackBerry, I'd crumble.

I've got a lot going on—I didn't even mention that I'm an active member of the Links, Delta Sigma Theta, and Jack and Jill—but I still try to take care of myself. I take time to get a mani-pedi every week and a half to two weeks. Always. And I'm on the massage table fairly regularly. I know it's important not to skimp on me.

Extreme Jobs

These jobs can have titles similar to those of the executive suite. Lawyers, journalists, bankers, agents, and even doctors can also work in the "extreme." An extreme job is really any high-level job that's been supercharged (see list on page 29). The cultural critic Catherine Orenstein described this phenomenon as the "American dream on steroids." These jobs, she has said, are an outgrowth of other societal extremes, everything from extreme, death-defying sports to the popularity of *Fear Factor*, *Extreme Makeover*, and other over-the-top reality shows.

In the workplace, extreme jobs are the high-risk, fast-paced, well-paid positions that now exist in nearly every industry. While highly demanding, important jobs are nothing new—and neither are the workaholics that fill them—these new jobs have been ratcheted up by globalization, technology, the rise of the workplace as social center, and our 24/7 cycle. They are for high-flying, overachieving road warriors who crave risk, power, excitement, and boatloads of money. These are, most visibly, the investment bankers, hedge fund managers, and consultants at top firms, such as Booz Allen Hamilton and McKinsey, who sign up for high levels of stress, extraordinary hours, an unpredictable schedule, global travel, and a corporate lifestyle in the "extreme."

Because many of these positions are in finance, during the most recent economic crisis—which brought about the failure of some high-level financial institutions—many extreme-level employees lost their jobs. Others were vilified. But these positions still exist and, as a result of restructuring, have become more extreme.

Dr. Sylvia Ann Hewlett, founding president of the Center for Work-Life Policy in New York, has written eloquently about the downsides of extreme jobs for women. She believes that the extreme-job work model excludes women, particularly those who either have families or want them. Two-thirds of the highly qualified female labor pool, she says, have serious family responsibilities.

In a 2006 *Harvard Business Review* article, "Extreme Jobs: The Dangerous Allure of the 70-Hour Workweek," which Dr. Hewlett wrote with Carolyn Buck Luce, the women offered snapshots of the extreme-job lifestyle. Working seven days a week and seeing family only on weekends was typical. So were getting a call in the middle of the night and hopping onto a flight to another time zone on short notice. Interviewees in Dr. Hewlett's book were forced to jump through hoops, like rearranging a wedding or a grandmother's funeral, to avoid missing meetings.

"Women simply don't get the same payoff from extreme jobs that men do," Dr. Hewlett writes. In other words, a man in an extreme job can have what Dr. Hewlett calls the "Triple Crown"—the great job, marriage, and kids. It's not the same for women. "For women, success in an extreme job might well threaten potential mates," she writes. "In addition, success at work may preempt children. It's awfully hard to both hold an extreme job and deal with the rigors of pregnancy, childbirth and mothering."

Still, some women choose to make these kinds of trade-offs. They have the passion, the drive, and the determination to make the extreme job environment work for them. Family, for them, might not be their first priority.

Others do it for a few years, make tons of money, and then leave to start families or work in less taxing environments. That's an option . . . if you survive.

—— WHAT IS EXTREME? ——

For her data analysis, Dr. Sylvia Ann Hewlett defined extreme jobs as those that require sixty hours or more per week, come with high salaries, and also feature at least five of these characteristics:

- Unpredictable flow of work
- Fast-paced work under tight deadlines
- Inordinate scope of responsibility that amounts to more than one job
- Work-related events outside regular work hours
- Availability to clients 24/7
- Responsibility for profit and loss
- Responsibility for mentoring and recruiting
- Large amount of travel

- Large amount of direct reports
- Physical presence at workplace at least ten hours per day

Extreme Job: Life in the Fastest Lane

To give you an idea of what the extreme lifestyle looks like, I spoke to a young woman who is a vice president in the investment area of a commercial bank. Previously she worked at a number of other large, well-known companies—Lehman, J.P. Morgan, Deloitte—in high-pressure positions. So she knows the territory very well. She describes her current job this way: "The managing directors and senior VPs win the business, get the deals. But I do the execution. They win it, my staff and I do it."

This woman, who is in her mid-thirties, asked that her name and company not be mentioned here, so that she'd be able to be brutally honest about what her career and life entail.

———————

Being a workaholic is pretty much what my job requires. And that's okay with me. Sleep has never been one of my top priorities. In college I worked full-time and then stayed up all night doing homework. I've never been interested in parties or doing the trendy thing. I like work.

I come into the office about 9:00 a.m., but I never know how long I'll have to stay. My philosophy is if I can leave on the same date, then I've had a good day. My job is fast-paced, and there's something to do all the time, every minute. Also, face time is really important. You are expected to adjust your personal life to the demands of the job. I could accomplish the same things at home, but who's going to see you at home?

When you get staffed on a pitch or are in the middle of a deal, things are even more crazy. At those times, everybody is a "CrackBerry" junkie. Numbers are flying, emails, faxes, phone calls, people have questions, there's something to review, you might have to go on a trip. I have to be available and on all the time.

At other times, there's still pressure. I cover an industry, so I have to keep current with news alerts, newspapers, and newsletters, not to mention building and growing relationships with people inside the company and in my industry.

My job is challenging, but it's also very creative. You can be thoughtful and innovative in how to structure a deal. We often work with companies that are suffering financially, especially in this economic climate. If you have the right ideas, you can make a huge difference. If you can think of a way to save a failing company—to make it stronger, literally rescue it—that's huge.

It's major when the deal closes. I love the celebratory dinner at a steakhouse with champagne. And the deal toy. Every time one of our deals closes, you get like a trophy. At the end of the day you want a shelf full of them.

Of course the money is a huge incentive. I didn't grow up with money. My mom was a teacher, and my father wasn't in the picture. In a good year, I can make $500,000. I paid more in taxes than all of my siblings made in income combined.

Unfortunately, since I don't have control of my time, I don't get to see them too much. I can't plan too far in advance, and I have to cancel plans all the time. I had a weekend planned for months, but I was asked to put something together for a Monday and had to cancel. I try to have as many friends outside work as possible, but it can be hard, especially when a lot of friends are from previous jobs. Most of us are taught to leave our personal lives at home. So it can be hard to get close. Why doesn't anybody talk about leaving your work life at work?

I do date, but it's a challenge. It's difficult to find someone who accepts that I don't have a lot of time. I could be working days straight, weeks, without a break. Even when I'm home, I'm working 24/7. A lot of guys can't deal with women who make more than them *and* have no time.

So if the money and excitement are the best parts, not having control of my time is the worst. I guess it's a trade-off you have to learn to balance.

—— CAREER PATH INVENTORY ——

Dr. Stella Nkomo, the coauthor of my first book, *Our Separate Ways*, and the director of research for ASCENT—Leading Multicultural Women to the Top, and I developed this simple tool to help women think about their career hopes and aspirations. If you go down any of the three paths unknowingly, you may end up disappointed. It's better to be mindful and intentional.

HOW IT WORKS

Read each statement and use the scale below to indicate how much you agree or disagree. There are no right or wrong answers; this is a thinking tool. So be as honest as you can, and be sure to respond to each item. Use the scoring guide to see where you stand. Then refer to the "What It Means" section to understand which career path is right for you.

HOW THE EXERCISE WILL AFFECT YOUR WORK LIFE

It will help you figure out where you're comfortable, what you're accustomed to, and how far you're willing to stretch. Once you identify the path best suited to you, with coaching and support you can come up with a strategy to get you where you want to go. Yes, there will be obstacles, but that's what this book is for—to offer insights and tools to help conquer them.

Remember, this instrument is a tool; nothing is set in stone. There may be times when you move between paths and strategies. If you want children or you're dealing with a sick parent, this may not be the time to pursue an extreme job. But keep your contacts, skill, and knowledge up to date, so that when you're ready to switch up, you'll be prepared.

Another thing: you might aim for the executive suite, not make it, and realize that you make a darn good corporate citizen. You can change your mind and your direction. The point is to help you be as intentional as you possibly can. It's fine to switch up. Each of these paths will also prepare you well for any entrepreneurial venture that you might be dreaming about.

SCALE

1	2	3	4
Strongly Disagree	Disagree	Agree	Agree Strongly

1. Making it home for the holidays is important for my well-being. _____
2. I am not concerned about having personal time for myself. _____
3. I enjoy traveling frequently for work. _____
4. I want to make big bucks. _____
5. Tight deadlines energize me. _____
6. I would rather work than go on vacation. _____
7. Work-life balance is very important to me. _____
8. I enjoy being focused on my work. _____

9. I get upset if I don't get personal time with my family each week. _____

10. I do not need to socialize with my friends often. _____

11. I am willing to be available to my clients anytime. _____

12. The faster the pace of work, the more I enjoy it. _____

13. Building a name and reputation for myself through a career is not one of my life goals. _____

14. I enjoy socializing with my work colleagues and bosses outside the workplace. _____

15. My career defines who I am in the world. _____

16. Attending work-related events outside work hours is not a problem for me. _____

17. I get a rush from meeting demanding deadlines. _____

18. I am willing to stay up all night to meet a work deadline. _____

19. I thrive under pressure. _____

20. Having power over others at work is not important to me. _____

21. I like having power over others at work. _____

22. I am willing to make as many sacrifices as are necessary to advance my career. _____

23. I want work but I do not want a demanding career. _____

24. It is important for me to be part of the team at work. _____

25. I am comfortable with having a corporate lifestyle. _____

26. I prefer to live in my ethnic community. _____

27. I do not like to socialize with colleagues after work. _____

28. I am willing to take risks at work. _____

29. I like to have a clear vision of what I am expected to accomplish at work. _____

30. I don't have to be the center of attention. _____

31. I easily bounce back from failure. _____

32. Taking on a global assignment and relocating would not be a problem for me. _____

33. I am comfortable networking with high-level executives and headhunters. _____

34. I go out of my way to take on tough assignments. _____
35. I am not interested in moving rapidly in a company. _____
36. I have demonstrated the ability to help my subordinates
    become leaders. _____

CAREER INVENTORY SCORING GUIDE

Instructions: Write in the score you chose for each of the questions
under the respective categories and then total each category.

Good Citizen Career Indicators

Question	Write in Your Score (1, 2, 3, or 4)
1. Making it home for the holidays is important for my well-being.	_____
7. Work-life balance is very important to me.	_____
9. I get upset if I don't get personal time with my family each week.	_____
13. Building a name and reputation for myself through a career is not one of my life goals.	_____
20. Having power over others at work is not important to me.	_____
23. I want a good job but I do not want a demanding career.	_____
24. It is important for me to be part of the team at work.	_____
26. I prefer to live in my ethnic community.	_____
27. I do not like to socialize with colleagues after work.	_____
29. I like to have a clear vision of what I am expected to accomplish at work.	_____
30. I don't have to be the center of attention.	_____

35. I am not interested in moving rapidly
    in a company.   _____

TOTAL SCORE   _____

Executive Suite Career Indicators

Question	Write in Your Score (1, 2, 3, or 4)

3. I enjoy traveling frequently for work.   _____

14. I enjoy socializing with my work colleagues
    and bosses outside of the workplace.   _____

15. My career defines who I am in the world.   _____

16. Attending work-related events outside work
    hours is not a problem for me.   _____

21. I like having power over others at work.   _____

22. I am willing to make as many sacrifices as are
    necessary to move up the corporate ladder.   _____

25. I am comfortable with having a corporate
    lifestyle.   _____

28. I am willing to take risks at work.   _____

31. I easily bounce back from failure.   _____

32. Taking on a global assignment and relocating
    would not be a problem for me.   _____

33. I am comfortable networking with high-level
    executives and headhunters.   _____

36. I have demonstrated the ability to help my
    subordinates become leaders.   _____

TOTAL SCORE   _____

Extreme Career Indicators

Question	Write in Your Score (1, 2, 3, or 4)

2. I am not concerned about having personal time for myself. _____

4. I want to make big bucks. _____

5. Tight deadlines energize me. _____

6. I would rather work than go on vacation. _____

8. I enjoy being focused on my work. _____

10. I do not need to socialize with my friends often. _____

11. I am willing to be available to my clients anytime. _____

12. The faster the pace of work, the more I enjoy it. _____

17. I get a rush from meeting demanding deadlines. _____

18. I am willing to stay up all night to meet a work deadline. _____

19. I thrive under pressure. _____

34. I go out of my way to take on tough assignments. _____

TOTAL SCORE

WHAT IT MEANS

Now examine your scores for each kind of career and answer—with thought and care—the following questions:

1. In which category is your score the highest? The category with the highest score indicates the type of career you currently prefer. You are more likely to be successful in whatever you do if the type of life and work experience you desire is in line

with the type of career you choose. If the scores are very close together (within two points), then you have some ambivalence about the type of career you prefer. You may want to look at the items associated with each type of career and reflect on the scores you assigned and why.

2. How accurate is your score? Does it reflect where you are now or want to be in your career?

3. If you are not where you want to be, what kinds of changes do you need to make?

BUILDING YOUR CAREER STRATEGY

Now that you have the data that you need, you can build your strategy for getting what you want. Below is a checklist to help you get started on your path or moving farther along it. If you're making a big midcareer switch, I've added a few extra things to do and think about. Give yourself time to really think these questions through, and write down the answers in your journal.

1. What are the strengths I have that will help me successfully pursue my path?

2. What areas do I need to develop?

3. Which assignments should I seek out?

4. Who are my role models? How can they be helpful to get me on my path and help me stay there?

5. Who would make a good mentor? How can my mentor assist me?

6. What other relationships do I need to develop? What alliances should I build?

7. What kind of additional education do I need? Would an MBA help?

8. Which professional groups should I be associated with?

If you're considering a midcareer change because you recognize that there are things you'd like to do differently, new paths to take, don't be afraid to reposition yourself inside or outside your company, in your industry, or in something brand-new. You owe it to yourself to at least try. Start by gathering as much information as you can to adapt to your own strategic plan.

1. What do I need to do to reposition myself?
2. How can my mentor help?
3. Do I need a coach, someone who can help from the outside?
4. I will talk to the people in my company who've succeeded on the path that I'd like to follow. I'll ask them: Who are their mentors, heroes, and sheroes? Where were they educated? What advice can they give me?
5. What's my brand? (Brand building will be discussed later in the book.) What am I known for now? Do people see me as a go-getter? Shy but hardworking? What do I want to be known for, and how does that align with the path I'd like to go on?

Choosing Your Career Path: The Essentials

- *Be mindful and intentional. Know who you are, and think about what you want to do and where you want to work.*
- *Think about the three career paths—good corporate citizen, executive suite, and extreme jobs—and consider which might be best for you and your particular*

personality and lifestyle. Our Career Path Inventory can help you sort through the specifics.

► *Create a career strategy. The to-do list you created in the "Building Your Career Strategy" section will help you get started on the path that's just right for you.*

What's Next?

This chapter discussed different kinds of jobs and career paths and how to identify which one might be right for you. I also asked you to create a navigating system—a list of strategies for helping you get to where you want to go. In the next chapter, we'll drill down and take a hard look at how the job search has changed, as well as offer the latest information on resumes, executive recruiting, interviewing, and where you need to look to find the position you want.

Chapter 3

The Twenty-First-Century Job Search

Globalization, technology, and the restructuring of most of the world's top corporations—not to mention the economy—have radically altered the way you find and secure the perfect job. If this is your first time looking for a "real job," you haven't changed jobs recently, or you've taken a break from the job market, you may need to get up to speed on the best ways to seek out and land the job you want.

Because the process has changed—and continues to change at a rapid pace—I reached out to several professionals for help: an executive recruiter, an author, several college career development professionals, and the head of a national career services association. They are in the trenches and know the trends in job search websites, resumes, the interview process, salary negotiation, and other fundamental elements of career management and change.

For simplicity's sake, I've organized this chapter into bite-sized chunks of how-to information, advice from the experts, suggestions, solutions, and everything else I could think of and dig up to help you find the position you want and deserve.

The Job Search Game: Doing It Right

One of my former students is exceptionally savvy when it comes to finding a job. She even managed to smoothly shift gears when her life took an unexpected turn in the middle of her job search. I asked her to share her story.

———————

I graduated from college in the late nineties with a degree in engineering and worked for about six years. I was a good engineer, but eventually I realized that I didn't have the business training to dig into the big issues. To be a good manager, I needed a broad-based perspective in marketing, finance, operations, and really all aspects of business so that I could make an impact across the areas of any company. So I applied to business school, and my husband did, too.

Because I was a more seasoned student with experience in the market, I knew that my job search needed to start even before I began classes. With the help of the career services office, I redid my resume. My goal was to keep it simple and brief and to focus on my skills and on the impact I had made, especially in money terms, such as reducing costs. I also translated the language of operations and engineering into English so that my experience in that field would be relevant to any industry.

Through the school, I also attended as many company briefings as I could. Since I wasn't sure where I wanted to work after graduation, I went to presentations about health care companies, consumer goods companies, investment banks, consulting firms, and even a manufacturer of heavy equipment. I wanted to work for an organization that I could feel good about, so I was especially attentive to the way the reps who visited talked about their organizations. Were they proud to work there? Did the company have integrity?

Other than that, I tried to meet as many people as I could. In school, I talked to other students like me, who had left their companies to go back to school. I had coffee with former venture capitalists, former directors of nonprofits, and ex-bankers to find out what they liked and didn't like and why they had left. Those people weren't selling their jobs, so it was easier to get honest information.

By the end of my first year, I had pretty much focused on working for an investment bank in sales and trading. I was interested in capital markets, a fast-paced day-to-day schedule, and an aggressive atmosphere. It seemed exciting.

I got a summer job at a major financial services firm, a company that was known for training people. I was very motivated, and by the end I had a very good understanding of the company and had learned what it was like to be in sales and trading. It seemed like a good fit for me.

Then things changed. I got pregnant at the end of my second year. The financial services firm offered me a position, but I couldn't commit. I knew what the demands of the job were, and knew it would be too much with a baby. Even if I was Superwoman and had full-time live-in care, I couldn't go in at 6:30 a.m. and work for twelve hours a day. So I had to say no.

I changed my job search and began to look at different fields. I needed to find a company and a job that offered me a rewarding, challenging career while also giving me the ability to get a young family off the ground.

I thought about consulting but was a little afraid of the travel. Finally, I settled on general management. It felt like a good fit—helping an organization in the day-to-day, from the inside, and working with people who might also have children. I also decided to focus on New York City, which had opportunities for both me and my husband.

At a networking dinner for women, I ended up at a table with a woman who ran a management development program at one of the country's leading publishing companies and some of my first-year classmates. During lots of lively conversation, I ended up letting the first-year women shine, and helped draw them out. The recruiter was impressed with me, seeing leadership potential. And I liked the company, which was well-known for making family a priority.

I graduated in 2007 and my son was born that year. I started at the publishing company not long after. As part of my rotational program, I've been in global strategy, worked with the CFO, and also been on a team that has redesigned the company's website. Because my job is like an internship, in another few months I'll have to find a permanent position, but in-house. That's fine; I've gotten very good at the job search.

GETTING STARTED

To find just the right position, you've got to use everyone and everything—friends, family, peers in your industry, mentors, former coworkers and classmates, professional organizations, alumni associations, and career development and placement professionals. Your quest is limited only by your own imagination and resourcefulness.

Increasingly, the Internet has become a power player in the job search game. Company websites, job search boards, and online social networks have replaced newspaper ads, which way back in the day were the main source of job listings. The Internet now contains millions of job postings across industries. Your goal is to find the websites and other online gatherings that best match your career aspirations. In general, online searches are most useful for recent college and business school graduates and current employees at the corporate citizen level. The cream of the crop—executive-suite positions and many of the extreme jobs—are generally handled by recruiters, either in-house or through a search firm or recruiter hired by the company.

I asked Lori Lorigo, associate director of the Tuck School of Business Career Development office, to explain how online job boards work and compile a list of the sites she recommends:

Online Job Boards

Online job boards have exploded in popularity over the past few years. Some boards are very general and have thousands of listings, while others target different audiences. The newer meta job search boards search other job boards and company websites online, and aggregate them into one search. In general, job boards offer prospective employees immediate access to real-time information and opportunities as well as the convenience of twenty-four-hour access and can point to positions in your area of the country. Most of the big sites allow you to fill out an online application, attach a resume, and click to send. The downside is that the cream-of-the-crop positions generally aren't listed on the large, general boards and probably aren't online at all. And sometimes because of the automation you may never receive a response of any kind—except for unsolicited junk mail, which has been a frequent complaint of users. However, job boards can be a good starting point.

General Online Job Boards

CareerBuilder: www.careerbuilder.com

Craigslist (classifieds and forums for more than 500 cities): www.craigslist.org

IMDiversity (serving people of color and women): www.im diversity.com

Job.com: www.job.com

Job Central: www.jobcentral.com

LatPro (for Hispanic and bilingual professionals): www.latpro .com

Monster.com: www.monster.com

Wall Street Journal's Career Journal: www.careerjournal.com

Yahoo! HotJobs: hotjobs.yahoo.com

Targeted to Recent College Grads

CollegeGrad.com: www.collegegrad.com

CollegeRecruiter.com: www.collegerecruiter.com

Targeted to MBAs

6 Figure Jobs: www.6figurejobs.com

Forte Foundation (for women): www.fortefoundation.org

Global Workplace: www.global-workplace.com

TheLadders.com: www.theladders.com

MBA-Direct.com: www.mba-direct.com

MBA-Exchange.com: www.mba-exchange.com

Meta Job Search Boards

Indeed.com: www.indeed.com

Juju: www.juju.com

Nushio: www.nushio.com

Simply Hired: www.simplyhired.com

Targeted to Specific Industries

Chronicle of Higher Education (academic jobs): http:// chronicle.com/jobs

Commongood Careers (social sector): www.cgcareers.org

Dice.com (technology): www.dice.com

eFinancialCareers: www.efinancialcareers.com

JobsInHealthCare.com: www.jobsinhealthcare.com

JobsInSports.com: www.jobsinsports.com

Justmeans (social enterprise): www.justmeans.com

MarketingHire.com: www.marketinghire.com

Opportunity Knocks (nonprofit): www.opportunityknocks.org

Private Equity Hub: www.pehub.com

RenewableEnergyJobs.com: www.renewableenergyjobs.com

Real-Jobs (real estate): www.real-jobs.com

WORKING YOUR ONLINE SOCIAL NETWORKS

If you've been joining social networking sites but spending most of your time uploading vacation photos—or if you've been hitting the delete button when friends and colleagues invite you to connect on a new online platform—you might want to start paying more attention. Especially if you're looking for a job.

Social networks, most prominently LinkedIn, have radically changed the old concept of networking and leveled the professional playing field. Gone are the days when networking meant handing someone a business card, sending your resume, following up with a phone call, and going in for an informational interview. The process has been streamlined so that you can meet other professionals through your network and stay in touch without seeing them offline or ever meeting them in the flesh. The people in your online network can give you a heads-up about openings, introduce you to others in their companies or networks, pass your resume along, and even hire you.

For tips on using social networking as a job search tool, I spoke to Marci Alboher, whose blog is called Working the New Economy (www.heymarci.com). She is also the author of the book *One Person/Multiple Careers: A New Model for Work/Life Success* (Warner Books).

LinkedIn has taken hold as the standard for most professionals, so link in. But you can also find networking opportunities on Facebook, MySpace, Orkut (created by Google), Spoke and Vidaeo (smaller versions of LinkedIn), Xing (international), and even Twitter. Keep up with the trade press in your field to figure out where your peers are congregating online, since niche communities are cropping up all the time. For example, Mediabistro.com is where media professionals hang out, and Lawyrs.net is the online spot for attorneys. Both feature industry news (and gossip), job listings, and workshops.

Give more than you ask for. Social networking sites— like old-fashioned in-person networking—are most effective when you build a reputation as someone who is a giver, rather than as someone who is always asking for favors. For example, if people in your network ask for help or introductions, check in periodically and respond when it's appropriate. If you've shown that you are a giver, you'll find that when you have a need to tap your network, people will be rallying to help you.

Find ways to use these sites to showcase your experience and achievements. If you have recently given a talk, published an article, or appeared on television, post a link describing what you did. Or start a blog, and feed your blog posts into the various social networks you're on.

Build your presence on these networks when you're not looking for a job. Make sure that your profile is up to date. Periodically check to see if there are people you know on the site that you could be connecting with. Be responsive to requests from your network. Also, don't wait for requests—for example, write unsolicited recommendations on Linked-In for colleagues whose work you admire. Should you then need to look for a new opportunity, your network will be well tended, and it won't be awkward to connect with people who can be of help.

A few words of caution:

When you create a presence on a social networking site, take the time to learn how to use it properly. If the site offers an online tutorial, take it. If possible, find a friend or colleague who is already part of the community to give you a primer on the site's etiquette.

Be mindful of your manners. Social networking sites make it easy to contact people, but in general, don't try to connect with people whom you don't know personally or whom you haven't been "introduced" to. Do not use these tools to spam anyone or to stalk people who haven't been responsive in other media. And make sure to review and follow the rules and guidelines of any community that you join.

SHOULD YOU USE AN EXECUTIVE RECRUITER?

At one point or other in your career, you may work with an executive recruiter or "headhunter" to help you find a job. Executive search firms are hired by companies and organizations to attract employees, generally at the higher leadership levels. These firms are paid by the companies who hire them to fill positions, typically at a fee of one-fourth to one-third of the job's first-year compensation. That money doesn't come out of your pocket; you pay nothing. Ideally, a recruiter can discuss your career development, refine your resume, point you to openings that aren't listed on job boards, get your resume to the right person, help prepare you for interviews, discuss whether you're the right fit, and assist with salary negotiation.

I asked Ellen Weber, executive vice president of Karen Tripi Associates (www.karentripi.com), a top New York City executive recruiting firm specializing in direct and digital marketing, for her input. Her blog, http://ellenweber.wordpress.com, has loads of posts that offer useful suggestions and tips about executive recruitment and the job search game.

Searches usually come in two types: retained and contingency. For a retained search, a company generally hires one firm to fill a specific position, typically at a very senior level. A firm working on a contingency search, on the other hand, is competing with other recruiters to find candidates to fill one or several jobs, generally midlevel or sometimes even junior positions. Contingency recruiters receive payment only when their candidate is hired.

If you plan to use a search firm, it's best to establish a relationship before you're looking. Recruiters are sometimes generalists, but more and more specialize. If you decide to use a search firm, ask around; find out who works in your industry and whom others in your field have used. A recruiter may reach out to you—or you can send your resume and let the firm know that you're interested in hearing about opportunities you might be appropriate for.

Success with an Executive Search Firm

Joyce Karel is chief marketing officer at Terra Sage, an online retailer for eco-friendly and healthy living products and services. She says that at her level, finding a new position involves so much more than just sending out a resume. When she was ready to look for a new job, she worked with Ellen Weber at Karen Tripi, but she also tapped her network of friends in the industry, including former coworkers, to help make the search process a success.

———————

My husband and I are both from the East Coast and had never planned to move to the Midwest. But in 2003, the perfect position came up at the Whirlpool Corporation in Benton Harbor, Michigan, and I knew I had to take it. I was offered the opportunity to build the company's relationship marketing and online advertising from the ground up for its North American brands. This position also gave me client-side experience, which I hadn't have before. My husband wanted to murder me, but I couldn't pass it up.

Four years later, both my husband and I were ready to get back to the East Coast. About that time Ellen Weber called me; someone I know had given her my name. It was perfect timing. I wasn't in a panic, but I was ready to leave.

Ellen and I talked about my career as a whole, and she helped me update my resume. Eventually, she connected me with Mullen Advertising, an Interpublic Group agency. The plan was that I'd work in their Detroit office for a year or so and then would be transferred to Mullen's office in Boston.

A year later, the plan changed. My husband had been launching a business and decided it was best if we moved to Chicago. First thing, I called Ellen. It helped that she had worked with me before and knew me. She helped me weed out positions that wouldn't be a good fit. The only meetings I went to were relevant and applicable to my experience and career goals.

Eventually, Ellen steered me to an opening at Ogilvy & Mather. Though she made the connection, I also reached out to people in my network. People say don't burn bridges, and it's true. Because of my network and connections, I knew many of the important players and knew a lot about the business. That made the process short. The interview was less about whether I could do the job, because they already knew that. It was more about chemistry and whether I was a good personality fit. In two weeks, I had an offer.

My husband and I ultimately decided it was time to move back to the East Coast to be close to family and friends. Again, Ellen played a key role in the search process and provided overall career guidance. We discussed the advantages and disadvantages of advertising agency versus client-side positions, as well as long-term professional and personal growth opportunities. In the end, the position at Terra Sage was the perfect fit.

I love my job, but I keep my resume updated and stay in touch with Ellen. It's an uncertain time and marketing is a volatile business, where things are constantly changing and people move around all the time. You never know.

THE RESUME REVISITED

Resumes have had a face-lift over the past decade. The old resume that simply lists jobs with short descriptions is dead. Your resume must reflect how you changed and influenced the process in a positive way and must be clear about your results and achievements. You have to take a hard look at the jobs you list and ask, "So what?" If you do that, your resume will change from a list of job descriptions to a document of achievement.

Your resume must also reflect more than just your basic skill set. In the past, if you were looking for a job in finance, that's what your resume would emphasize. But now that companies have flattened and there is less middle management, leadership and teamwork are important. You must now be able to show how you worked on a team or, even better, led a team, and discuss the results you achieved. If you've worked across different areas—finance, marketing, *and* sales—all the better.

And, increasingly, companies are looking for something global: you were part of an exchange program or internship in college, you speak another language, or at a previous job you ran a unit in another country. The minimum is that you are well traveled or that you worked for a company that did business worldwide. But it's essential that you have some kind of global orientation.

In a tough economy, make sure your resume is recession-proof. Emphasize ways you contained and cut costs, generated revenue, and increased productivity and efficiency. Be as specific as you can, using actual dollar figures, percentages, and before-and-after comparisons. At the same time, stress your resourcefulness and flexibility, using specific examples when at all possible. Show that you were able to adapt to expanded responsibilities. Explain how you led your team through tough times or initiated and completed a successful turnaround.

Finally, if you're submitting your resume online—either to a company website or to an online job board—you should assume that it will be entered into an applicant tracking system. This electronic gatekeeper sorts resumes by skills based on key words. Keywords are typically nouns but may also include verbs that reflect skills and experience sought by a potential employer. Think buzzwords. So to be most effective, reshape your resume to include the skills, industry terminology, and education that would be most important to the type of position you are seeking. Some general keywords that stand out: "strategic planning," "performance and productivity improvement," "organizational design," "team building," "new media," "e-commerce," "problem solving," "leadership," "cost reduction," and "competitive market." Don't be afraid to put them right at the top of your resume. For guidance, take a look at the sample resume on the next page. Strong, relevant, and active key words are right at the top. Note how the key terms are woven into the body of the resume. Each section amplifies at least one or two of those terms.

As you write your own resume for posting, think of your key words almost as web links: highlights of your background that will bring recruiters and potential employers to you.

J .L. Williams
1 Erehwon Place • New York, NY 10055
(555) 555-5555
0000JL@gmail.com

*Good
key words that pop*

**Art Buying/Creative Management • Global Print Production • Process
Implementation and Improvement • New Business Coordination • Cost
Containment and Reduction • Team Building and Leadership**

*Bold,
positive
description of skills
and talents with good
key words, including
international*

Highly motivated results-driven manager of people and projects in a fast-paced environment. Go-to person for outsourcing creative materials for international presentations. Big-picture supervisor with an eye for details that, if overlooked, could lead to costly mistakes. Strong leader with an ability to motivate people to achieve future goals in a timely manner.

The Intergalactic Group   **April 2000 to Present**
Manager of Creative Services
(accounts include XYZ Company, JKL Inc., and FGH Corp.)
Manage, coordinate and negotiate photographers, models, illustrators, art directors, copywriters, designers, retouchers, and production vendors for international creative presentations. Manage budget and implement cost reduction and containment strategies.

*Description
of job highlights
promotions and
achievements, clients,
and key words*

Key Achievements:
- Led creative team through transition from traditional advertising to event planning
- Coordinated a team from across all areas of the company to update and rebrand the company website and new media presentations
- Developed system for assigning and completing presentation and production materials, containing departmental costs
- Selected to participate in company leadership training program

*Emphasizes
leadership, cost
reduction/containment,
ability to cross department
borders, technology*

Education
Columbia University
Magna cum laude, Bachelor of Arts, minor in Spanish

International

New York University
Master of Business Administration, internship with Momentous World Wide, Barcelona office, 2000

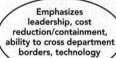

International

CRASHING THE ELECTRONIC GATE

In many if not most companies, particularly for midlevel positions, you may be asked to fill out an electronic application after you submit your resume. This prescreening tool helps companies select candidates who are worth a face-to-face interview. You might be asked general questions about salary requirements, how many work days you've missed in the past year, and whether you're willing to relocate. Other companies test potential employees by asking more detailed questions or having them analyze a case study to access skills and knowledge beyond what's on the resume. You might be required to fill out a behavioral assessment, for example, to determine your strengths in terms of teamwork or negotiation.

Here are some tips to help you prepare for online prescreening:

- Tell the truth. Don't exaggerate your skills or knowledge; overinflating what you've got can catch up to you, even in your next step—the interview.
- Keep your resume in front of you while you're filling out the electronic form to ensure consistency.
- Don't leave a lot of answers blank. That might look suspicious.
- Take your time. It's best to be thoughtful and truthful.
- Keep a copy of the information you submitted by printing the pages.

NAIL THE INTERVIEW

Technology has altered the job search. Your interview, however, will still be conducted by a live human being, and it will probably be a fairly rigorous affair. There is really no such thing as an informational interview; that's a thing of the past. Your level of preparation and knowledge has to be much higher. You've got to do your homework. Sitting across from an interviewer, you'd better know what the company is and does, its place in the larger market, where its offices are, other companies it's partnering with, and what you can contribute. Thanks again to technology, that is information you can get your hands on quickly.

The interviewer will also be trying to get a feel for you and your personality, to help figure out if you'd be a good fit. Remember, too, that an interview is a two-way street. You should ask questions to assess whether you want the job, if you want to work for the company, if you'd be happy there, and if you fit into the corporate culture.

We asked our experts for more advice on getting the interview right:

- **Do the research.** Learn all you can about the company or organization so that both your questions and answers during the interview will be sophisticated and knowledgeable. Know the job you're interviewing for. If you aren't prepared, the interviewer will assume you're not serious about the position or that you're uninterested in getting it.

- **Know what's on your resume.** You should be clear about where you worked and when and what you did. Bring a copy, but don't look down at it as you speak. That will make you seem unprepared and scattered. If you have a gap in your work history, tell the truth about it. Explain that you took time off to raise your child or take care of your ailing father.

Also describe any classes you took, freelance assignments, or volunteer work you did during that time.

- **Have your elevator speech prepared.** What do I mean by "elevator speech"? It's a short dialogue you can pull out when you get an opportune moment to connect with a senior executive. (I'll discuss this in more detail in Chapter 5.) During an interview, a short, prepared speech gives the impression that you're knowledgeable about the company, you have good ideas, and you're looking for ways to contribute. It's not the time to complain or give your five cents about what's going wrong. It should be tight and concise, explaining why you want the job and why the interviewer should take you seriously. Look for ways to emphasize leadership, teamwork, results, technology, international experience, ability to function outside of your particular "silo," and anything else you have that the company might want.

- **Do a run-through.** You can't predict everything, but practice the major points you'd like to hit—with a friend, in front of a mirror, to your dog.

- **Arrive early, ten or fifteen minutes before schedule.** Be observant. This is a great opportunity to play anthropologist, to see what you can learn about the culture, and to pick up signals or clues about the company. Don't you dare be even one second late. Enough said.

- **Treat all people you encounter with professionalism and kindness.** Be respectful and professional with the interviewer, even if he or she acts casual. And remember that the receptionist or administrative assistant may offer his or her opinion of you to the boss. It could count.

- **Dress appropriately.** If you aren't sure about the company dress code, use your network to figure out what to wear or make a quick call to the receptionist beforehand. Overdress rather than underdress. Even if people are in jeans, don't you do it. And avoid anything provocative or overdone. You want to look stylish but appropriate.

- **Sell yourself well.** Project a combination of intensity and thoughtfulness, confidence and enthusiasm. If you're too low-key or lack energy, it may look like you're not really interested. Avoid seeming aggressive, pushy, or egotistic.

- **Be prepared to discuss salary.** Do research to determine the going rate. Have in mind a fair salary range for the job you're discussing so that you'll be ready when money comes up. Websites such as Salary.com and SalaryExpert.com offer very detailed information for free. Most companies will want to know your current salary, and, increasingly, they are asking for W-2 forms. So it's best to tell the truth.

- **Don't disrespect the company you work for.** Have a good reason why you want to leave your current job. It shouldn't be "I hate my boss." Stick to the positive. Say, "I'm looking for opportunities to grow."

- **As the interview winds down, understand the employer's next step—and yours, too.** When should you expect to hear something? Always thank the interviewer, shake hands firmly, and make eye contact.

- **After you leave, jot down notes so you remember the key points and details.** If you're working with a search firm, call your recruiter and tell him or her how it went.

- **Follow up with a note right away.** Not an email, but a handwritten thank-you on nice stationery. It should be short and graceful, expressing gratitude for the interviewer's time and reiterating your interest in the position.

- **If you really want the job, go the extra step.** Follow up by sending an article or piece of research on something you talked about during the interview.

- **If you haven't heard back in the time frame indicated by the interviewer, it's fine to call and check in.** Just be careful not to stalk.
- **Negotiate well.** If you're offered the job, in most cases you'll need to settle on the salary, benefits, and other goodies. For tips on negotiating wisely, see Chapter 6.

FINDING A JOB IN A DOWN MARKET

Just because the economy slows down doesn't mean your job search has to grind to a halt. But you may have to be a little more imaginative than when the economy is on the upswing.

First and foremost, don't panic, says Marilyn Mackes, the executive director of the National Association of Colleges and Employers (NACE; www.naceweb.org), a professional membership organization located in Bethlehem, Pennsylvania. Panic and desperation fuel only more panic and desperation. Take a deep breath and feel confident that you will find a job, one you enjoy. And remember that there is no typical career path anymore. Your path isn't going to be a straight line; it'll be curvy, with lots of twist and turns.

NACE forecasts trends in the job market, and Mackes particularly tracks legal issues in employment and hiring. She offers some tips for navigating the job market during difficult or uncertain economic times:

Do the work. In a tough market, it's even more important to do everything right. So make sure your resume is clear and truly highlights your skills, talents, achievements, and results. Work your network, online and off. Now's not the time to be shy about reaching out and asking for guidance and direction. Do your homework and thoroughly research the industry, the market, and any company you're interested in.

Highlight skills that are valuable in a down market. For example, experience with budgets and cost management is necessary in difficult economic times. Show that you can manage and even inspire people under fire. Offer examples of ways you're worked effectively when resources are tight. Make extra sure to highlight points like these on your resume.

Think outside of your own box. Look at yourself and what you have to offer in a different light. Just because you've always worked in operations doesn't mean that's all you can do. Think about other ways to describe who you are and what you have. Are you a natural leader who heads the diversity committee at your current job? Do you have accounting skills from working at your parents' grocery store growing up? Are you highly organized and the recording secretary of your church or temple's board of directors?

Be flexible. Consider what there is a demand for and position yourself toward that demand. With a finance background or MBA, you might have your sights set on Wall Street. But a job in health care or energy might be a better option, depending on what's going on in the world and the market. Maybe you had planned to work for a large, well-known corporation, but your skills might be attractive to a smaller company or even a nonprofit or the government. Keep your geographic options open. Living in New York or Chicago might be your dream, but think about a smaller city in the Midwest or the South instead.

The Twenty-First-Century Job Search Essentials

- *Pursue every avenue. Now's not the time to be shy about reaching out to friends, family, peers, former coworkers, professional organizations, and placement professionals.*
- *Search online job boards. Careerbuilder.com, Monster .com, and many other job boards have grown in popularity. Include them in your toolbox.*
- *Use social networking sites, most prominently LinkedIn. This is the modern way to network your way into a job.*
- *Consider using an executive recruiter. Headhunters are valuable, especially at the higher levels.*
- *Keep your resume up to date. It should be a document of achievement, reflecting more than just your basic skill set and a list of past jobs.*
- *Come to an interview ready to discuss what the company does, where it fits in the market, and how you can contribute. Then stay relaxed and be authentic.*
- *Be flexible when looking for a job in a down market. Try not to be discouraged. You will find the job you deserve.*

What's Next?

In the chapter that follows, I will discuss what to do once you've landed the job and you're ready to begin. The first ninety days in a new position are critically important. I'll help you create a plan of action so you can hit the ground running.

Chapter 4

Hit the Ground Running: Your First Ninety Days on the Job

Not long ago, one of my former students got an exciting, high-paying job offer in the New York real estate industry. Though this was a great opportunity for her, she would have to relocate from Chicago, out of her comfort zone, and into a highly visible position at a company that didn't have a great track record for women. But I thought she could and should do it. She was very smart, with an extraordinary knowledge base about the industry, and she also had business savvy as well as street sense. Highly determined, she was also grounded, took good care of herself, had a good support system, and knew when to ask for help.

Before she started, I offered her this advice: "In such a high-profile, visible job, you've got to ascend. If you screw up, the whole world's going to know. Make your mark right away—in the first ninety days. It's okay to make mistakes once they get to know you, but at the outset, in the first ninety days, there's no room for error. So do everything as close to target as possible."

As we designed her game plan, she was hungry to know more. I explained that in the first three months, she needed to quickly understand her company's culture, figure out what was expected of her, connect with her manager, and learn who the power players were. It was also important for her to learn where her business fit in the larger industry and be aware of competitors. At the same time, I suggested she solidify her external network and build in time to hang out with people who care about her, in order to avoid burnout.

I was proud of her: She followed the game plan and made a big name for herself. Ten years ago, a woman wouldn't have been offered a job like this. This woman, though, not only held on, she soared. She had a plan, and she stuck to it.

In our fast-paced world, the first three months at a new job are critical. This holds true for all jobs, right up to the president of the United States. Your colleagues are watching, and they form their opinions very quickly, particularly for women, and especially women of color. That means you have no time to waste: either you figure out the lay of the land and prove you're a leader by making some strategic decisions, executing a plan, and showing some results or the buzz about you and what you bring to the table will quickly diminish and you'll have to work even harder to prove your worth. The more quickly you get clear about who's who and what's what, the better your chance of success. These first ninety days are truly the time to hit the ground running.

DECODING THE COMPANY CULTURE

Every workplace, whether corporate, academic, or not-for-profit, has its own culture. And you need to figure out the cultural landscape in the first three months.

When I came to the Tuck School of Business, I'd been at several Ivy League schools. I thought I knew how to handle myself. I'd done it before. But every culture has its quirks. What I learned here was that at Tuck, face time is more important than at other schools. You can't just teach or hole up in your office grading papers and doing research. You have to attend events and socialize with colleagues. Hanover, New Hampshire, is a small village with a close-knit community. So you have to be comfortable seeing your colleagues, students, and boss outside of work—at the gym or when you're shopping or just hanging out. I learned pretty quickly that here they need to see you.

Some companies help out by providing "on-boarding," a process designed to help new employees get socialized and become an active part of the corporate community. But most companies don't do a very good job at this. They don't explain the company's norms, help you figure out how you fit in, or introduce you to people. They might not even tell you where the bathroom is. They throw you into the water and expect you to swim with all the other fish, including sharks. Another way to put it is that you're expected to jump onboard the fast-moving company train with no conductor. This is true at all levels, whether you're coming in as a newbie or you have a lot of experience and have been recruited because of your knowledge, wisdom, and track record. Even if you're just moving to a different part of the company, to a different product line or functional group, or to a different location, the clock restarts. It's your first ninety days all over again.

One of your first tasks as a new hire should be to deconstruct the organizational culture in order to fit into the corporate community. Culture is that invisible glue that holds all the behaviors, values, norms, heroes and sheroes, and traditions together. In other words, it's the air you breathe at work. You can't see it, but it's an extremely powerful force that shapes everyday life—including patterns, behaviors, communication, and relationships at any company. Along with the more obvious formal culture, every company also has a collection of unwritten rules, behaviors, and activities.

This "informal culture" is something you'll also need to decode, the sooner the better. You'll need to read between the lines to figure out, for instance, who has the most power and authority. Hint: it might not be the manager with the fancy title; it could be his secretary. In other cases, the most powerful person may be a peer who's responsible for delegating and distributing assignments or resources. He's not your boss, but he can give you the worst assignments in the tightest, most stressful time frames—or he can work with you and make your life more manageable. Remember, you don't have power over these people, so you have to find a way to influence them in some way. It requires relationship building, which we'll discuss in depth in Chapter 5.

Every company's culture, both formal and informal, is different. If you did your homework before you took the job, you've gotten some information and have learned about the culture of the company. The culture at PepsiCo, for example, is young, upbeat, high-energy, and cool. It's a think-out-loud culture, very different from bank culture; think Pepsi Generation. Working there requires you to be analytical as well as social, both within the company and in the larger community. But what do you do if you're a little older, shy, or reflective? You've got to come up with your own way to navigate this unique culture.

Assessing the culture and how to fit in can be tricky. Too often, people are so busy trying to figure out company norms, how to interact with administrators, and even whom to interact with that their performance diminishes. That's why you need to understand what the job requires, develop the know-how to navigate the culture, establish relationships, identify resources, and prioritize what's important. In other words, you need to get the job done.

KEEP A JOURNAL

In general, you're not in high-action mode during the first ninety days. You're in observation mode. Put your ear to the ground and record what you hear; what you find out will help you crack the corporate culture code. Also take note of what you're feeling and how you're doing.

The easiest way is by keeping a journal. But it shouldn't just be a cold, distant record of your corporate endeavors. Write down as much as you can, including your feelings—when you got excited, when you felt that sinking feeling in the pit of your stomach.

Always carry your journal with you. Don't leave it on your desk. If it's not with you, keep it in a locked file cabinet, and never on your work computer. Your opportunities, resources, and observations about individuals should go in your journal, and that's not public information. It's best to take your journal home and do a dump onto your home computer every night—and make sure your home computer isn't connected to your office in any way, shape, or form. Here's what you should take note of:

Who are the heroes?
Who seems to have power?
Who's the "golden child"?
Who are the underdogs?
Where are the underdogs?
Who interacts with whom, and how and where?
Which people have lunch together?
Which people take smoking breaks together?
Who winds up going out to run, play basketball, shop? Who
    hangs with whom?
How do people dress?
What are the burning issues?

How is competition talked about?

If a big person has a lot of power, who helps get things done?

Who seems to take all the credit for everyone else's success?

At meetings, do they come with food? Are people using Black-
Berrys during the meeting or not?

Do people answer emails after standard work hours?

Do people socialize in meetings or just come in, take the
meeting, then disperse?

Do they hang out at the water cooler or is it work all the time?

Do they discuss vacations? Or do you have the impression that
they work all the time?

What time do they come in? What time do they leave?

What does success look like? When there's a successful
project, what does that look like?

Whom can you trust?

When there's a failure, what does that look like?

Getting the Lay of the Land

*Krystal Williams is a program manager for the Agricultural and Turf
Division, Strategic Manufacturing, at John Deere. She's a smart, am-
bitious young woman whom I met while she was studying for her
MBA at Tuck.*

*In 2003, Krystal began as a marketing manager at Deere's office
in North Carolina, not far from where she grew up. But two years
later, when her manager left, she was transferred to the company's
world headquarters in Moline, Illinois. Though her new position was
in the same company—a global corporation with more than fifty thou-
sand employees—she had to start the ninety-day on-boarding process
all over again, in a new city.*

When I started in January I came in with a project and immediately started to formulate a tactical plan to get it completed. This tactical plan was what I needed for the day-to-day, until I could come up with a long-term strategy.

My first goal was to meet the key players. Since I had already established some relationships, I was able to rely on the network of people who trusted my business and intellectual acumen. I am a very friendly person, so I also wasn't shy about going into the company's organization chart and setting up informational sessions to find out the lay of the land. I sent emails to people and introduced myself. The notes sounded like this: "Hi, I'm Krystal Williams, and I'm working on a project to better understand customer drivers for and the use of hybrid electric technology in our equipment. I think this has a specific benefit in your area. Can we get together to discuss concerns and opportunities? I hope you don't mind my being forward, but I'd like to put thirty minutes on your calendar."

I was clear that I wanted to give each person the opportunity to tell me first what they didn't like about my ideas; that way, the issue was on the table and I could address it. I also selected the times carefully. I asked for thirty minutes but tried to schedule times on their electronic calendar when I could see that they actually had an hour free! It was the business equivalent of going out for coffee on a date.

In the course of a month and a half, I had coffee with a smattering of people, maybe six or seven, most of them at the product planner or director level. I went to decision makers; everyone was above me. These meetings gave me a sense not just of what was going on but also of who the influencers were, what they were thinking, and what questions they needed me to answer in order for me to gain their support.

In the end, my project didn't move forward. But down the road, those early meetings mattered. Everything came full circle. One of the people I had met with remembered me and appreciated the work I had shared with him. That led to my current job, which is high-level and very strategic; I report to a director.

Another crucial lesson that I learned from those early coffee meetings was that it was good that I came to these leaders—who happened to be all men—with a problem: how do I move my project ahead? I didn't do this intentionally, but men typically like to solve problems. It was a good icebreaker and made the conversations easy.

BRAND YOU

In your first three months, you must create your reputation and tell people who you are. You have to be in control of defining yourself, rather than allowing people to define you. You want them to walk away with the image you are projecting. You want them to know your "brand." Ideally, it might be something like this: "She is straightforward; she knows her stuff; she knows relationships are important; she's clear about what she's doing and what she needs in order to get it done." Most important for women, and especially women of color, your colleagues at all levels must think, "She's a team player."

What's a brand? *Branding* is a marketing term. A good brand is a product or service that you don't forget, that you want to use, that you always go to, that you trust. Think back to the brands you still remember from childhood: You're in good hands with Allstate. KFC—we do chicken right. Heinz, the slow ketchup. Timex keeps on ticking. Nobody doesn't like Sara Lee.

Why is brand important to your career, particularly during your first ninety days at any job? Your brand is the image that conveys your strengths, what you're known for, what makes you truly unique, how people will continually remember you. It's an unforgettable image of you that pops into someone's mind. In essence, it's your reputation and your corporate persona. You must establish a strong brand the second you walk through a company's door.

As a professor, I've established this brand: *I'm wise, but still cool enough to connect with students. I'm savvy and stay current about how people think about leadership right now. I'm a good storyteller. And I know when to tell someone to cut the crap. I'm passionate, energetic, and even loud. I don't want my students to look at me with dead-fish eyes. And I'm caring.* That's my brand. I know because I've asked my students. And those are the things that they tell me consistently. I've worked hard to build my brand. Building a brand takes time. It comes from honing those behaviors and skills that you're really good at and also stretching in those areas where you need to grow—the skills and behaviors you might not be as comfortable with.

As you shape your brand, you need to be as authentic as possible. Too often a corporate persona or brand is built on ego—what the ego makes us think will be big, bad, and wonderful—rather than who we really are. Brands that work and which people remember are built on your values and your authentic self.

Think of President Obama. His brand is in sync with his personality; there's no cognitive dissonance between the two. His persona is cool. He doesn't get angry easily. He lets go of baggage. He's able to listen to diverse and contrary views. He builds alliances. I suspect this has to do with who he is as a man; it's part of his value set, not an invention that he pulled out of the sky. That's why it works.

If you aren't sure about your brand, ask someone who knows you, who's worked with you. This will allow you the opportunity to shape your brand during the first ninety days. Ask questions like "How do people see me? "What two words would you use to describe me?" Then listen with an open mind to their answers. Don't get defensive if it's not how you would describe yourself.

Once you establish a great brand, people have to talk about it. That's called buzz. It's a good thing if in your first three months at a job—or any time—there's a buzz around the company about what you do, how you do it, and what your brand is. Not long ago, I had breakfast with the new vice president of diversity at Dartmouth. Although we had never met, in the first five minutes I could tell she already knew exactly who I was. First thing she said was, "I've heard so many good things about you, and everything I hear is wonderful." That's good buzz.

Good buzz means that when your name is mentioned, people say good things about you. They're talking about you and want to be associated with you. You'd be surprised how that opens doors. When there's an opportunity, especially early on, and people are brainstorming—"Who would be good at this?"—they might hear the buzz about you and your brand and might think of you. You might not have the experiences in that area, but because your brand has integrity, they believe you can do it. A good brand really showcases your talent, wisdom, and leadership. Based on your brand and buzz, someone might take a risk on you or look out for you when the company's downsizing.

Mentors, role models, and allies can help you create good buzz. (I'll talk much more about relationships in the next chapter.) At best, when they aren't working and interacting with you, they're talking about you in a good way. After a face-to-face with you, they go into meetings, send email to other people, and participate in conference calls. They talk about what they're doing and whom they're working with—and they include you. They become part of your fan club.

A note of caution: There's good buzz, bad buzz, and so-so buzz. Of course, avoid bad buzz. It sounds like this: "She's hard to work with, doesn't follow through, is always late, creates drama." There's also the so-so buzz: no excitement, no energy. That's just about as deadly as bad buzz. It doesn't say anything about you.

SIDESTEPPING STEREOTYPES

If you define yourself clearly and establish a solid brand early, you can manage the invisible stereotypes that are dancing around like ghosts in any and every workplace. Though women have been an integral part of the professional labor force since the 1970s, we are still plagued by gender stereotypes. Women of color often must shoulder the added burden of racial, ethnic, and cultural stereotyping.

To be clear, most of these stereotypes are unintentional. It's not sexism or racism per se. It's a natural, subconscious categorizing process. It's coded into the language, and it affects how we see each other and how we describe people. And it's not just white men who carry these images; all of us carry them of each other as well.

The thought process goes, "I don't know anybody like you, and so I need to put you in a box or connect you with someone I do know. It could be someone who's in the movies, who took care of me as a child, who cleans my house, who delivers Chinese food, or whom I met at a resort in Jamaica."

The idea that all women are too emotional is a stereotype that gets us into trouble. It's not that you shouldn't show you have emotions. But the stereotype is that women are caring and emotional at the expensive of being firm and decisive.

Black women, specifically, are often stereotyped as "angry." Those who have a serious demeanor and don't walk around smiling or hang out with associates after hours can get categorized as "angry black women," or ABWs. If you dig deeper, the image of the ABW is akin to the Sapphire stereotype, that wisecracking, hostile, demeaning black character who first came to life in the *Amos and Andy* series. Unfortunately, she's still alive. (If you don't believe me, think about the stereotype that Michelle Obama briefly struggled with on the campaign trail as the angry, hostile black woman no matter how much she smiled.) Being branded as an ABW is code for "doesn't work well with others," "not a team player," "not a good leader."

White women are sometimes stereotyped as competitive, looking out only for number one. Hard-driving, ambitious white women, those who are very bright but not chummy, are seen as "queen bees." Or they might be labeled "Annie Oakleys," frontier women with their finger on the trigger, loners who can take care of themselves. This stereotype is corporate code for "not a team player," "not trustworthy," "won't watch your back, but will probably stab it."

Asian women can get trapped in the stereotype of passivity, the notion that they don't speak up. Chinese and Japanese women in particular are easily branded with having very low emotional intelligence skills and often aren't perceived as leadership material. This is connected to their cultures, where it's important to reflect before you speak and make decisions. If you're thoughtful and reflective, your voice might not always be heard. But this doesn't mean you can't be an effective leader.

The best way to avoid stereotyping? Control your brand and create positive buzz in the first ninety days and throughout your career. Define who you are rather than allowing others to do it for you.

ESTABLISHING RELATIONSHIPS

Establishing and leveraging strategic relationships is more important during your first ninety days than at any other point in the life span of your job. How well you do it can make or break your career at the company. Unfortunately, strategic relationships are an area that women frequently have trouble managing. We reason, "I'm putting my nose to the grindstone and working as hard as I can. Why do I need to be friendly to these people or socialize with them when I'm proving myself by doing my job well?"

The truth is, you need people. It's crucial for you to seek out advice and help both inside and outside the company. Inside, there are people at every level to give you the lay of the corporate landscape, to help you understand who's who, what's what, and how the company ticks.

Outside the company, your peers, former coworkers, friends, and family can offer support, including emotional support, as you find your way in a new job. You might just need someone to pray and meditate with. If you haven't already, create a "kitchen cabinet." This is a group of women and men with good experience whom you can run things by. They can help you makes sense of what's going on, clarify your thinking, and push you beyond your comfort zone. If your position is very senior and the stakes high, you might invest in a coach to help you sift through what's going on and figure out a plan. (I'll give you more information about coaching in Chapter 7.)

As you establish internal relationships in the first ninety days, seek out people at all levels, not just with the upper-ups. When I first arrived at Dartmouth, I learned that mentors come with many faces. Early on, I had to submit a proposal for research monies. At other schools I'd been at, faculty didn't ask for a lot of money, since no one got it. So I asked for a pittance. When I gave my proposal to my assistant, Pat, to type up, I was very formal; I'm sure I had an air of arrogance. She *was* support staff, after all.

The next morning, she wiggled her finger at me and pointed to a chair. "Come here, sit down," she said. At first I thought, *You can't be talking to me like this!* but I sat down. She handed the proposal back to me and said, "You don't want to submit this. If you do, you aren't going to have enough money to do what you need to do this year. None of your colleagues submit in this range," she added. "You have enough documentation in terms of your work plan to support a bigger request." She gave me a new number and said, "This is more appropriate and in the range of your colleagues. You have a choice. You can do it your way or my way." Needless to say, I did it her way, and learned an important lesson about relationships.

People also need to have a sense of who you are. This makes many women nervous; we want to present a professional front and not be stereotyped as too personal or intimate, which feels inappropriate at work. But it's exactly when people don't know who you are that you get slapped with a stereotype. And when people don't know who you are, they aren't sure if they can trust you. If I'm in a track meet and I'm going to hand off a baton to you, I need to know that you are going to grab it, and also that you aren't going to drop it or run in the wrong direction. People have to have a sense of you in order to know that you are going to run with the baton. That kind of trust comes from knowing a person.

In the next chapter, I will discuss relationships in depth. But for now, in the first ninety days, make sure you have these key meetings, along with informally getting to know others. (If you don't know exactly what to say, don't worry; later on I'll explain how to create a "script.")

1. **Meet with your manager or managers.** At least have coffee. Introduce or reintroduce yourself, then ask where he or she believes the company is headed and what needs to be done. During this meeting, you must clarify what your objectives are, particularly around your first assignments. What are the critical things he or she sees you doing? The higher up you go, the more vital this is. You also need to be clear about what resources you need—human, financial, technological, and logistical—to accomplish these goals.

2. **Get to know your team.** These are the people who work with you, collaborate with you, and report to you. These are the people who help you get your product delivered and look good. Do some fact-finding by peeking at their Facebook pages, listening to the buzz, or, even better, asking them about themselves. When you meet with your team, find out what condition they're in. What's been the prior experience? Where is the team at present? What are their expectations of you? What are your expectations of them? What do they need to look good so that you can look good? Establish lines of authority and communication. How does information flow—by email, or with daily check-ins?

3. **Meet key stakeholders.** Invite them to have coffee, or offer to bring them an afternoon latte. Begin to establish relationships. That's called managing up. Make sure to tell your immediate supervisor what you're doing.

The Gym Is the New Golf Course, and Other Informal Networking Strategies

Trudy Bourgeois is the founder and president of the Center for Workforce Excellence, a company that focuses on providing individuals and organizations with ideas and solutions to bring out their best performance. The author of several books, including The Hybrid Leader: Blending the Best of the Male and Female Leadership Styles, *she has thoughtful views on leadership and career development.*

Rather than the first ninety days of a new job, she believes in the one-hundred-day framework. "The first one hundred days comes from the length of time a new president of the United States is given to gather analysis, build strategy, and announce, 'This is what's going to happen under my watch,'" says Trudy. "But whether you're a CEO or you sweep the floors at night, the first few months of your job set the stage for what's to come."

I asked Trudy for some ideas to help make your first ninety days a success. Here is what she suggests.

————————

As early as you can, figure out the minicultures within the larger culture. The best way to do this is by socializing outside of work, when everybody's game face is removed and their hair is down. You'll learn about the informal way business gets done, you'll see informal mentoring, and you'll learn stuff that people won't necessarily say in public.

Often this happens on the golf course. But don't worry if you don't play. The gym is the twenty-first-century golf course. Whenever you're in a work-related social setting, be strategic; this isn't a time to get your drink on. Many a career has been damaged if not destroyed because people didn't have the savvy to display leadership at a cocktail party, company dinner, or weekend retreat. Show that you can you handle yourself outside the work environment as well as inside. They aren't going to be sending you to London if you're drunk over dinner.

Etiquette is very important and depends on your company's culture. So even when you don't know, act like you do. At a formal dinner, for example, find one person to focus on who knows how things work. Still, be authentic and genuine; be yourself.

DEVELOPING YOUR SCRIPT

What's your script? It's a way to communicate who you are and how you want to be seen in a nutshell. It's the corporate persona that you create, and which you control. Your script is what makes you special and unique. It helps you establish relationships with people, especially early on, and it allows people to know something about you—who you are as a person. It helps others connect the dots.

Having a script makes it easier for people to get a sense of you and is especially useful if you're uncomfortable talking about yourself in encounters and interactions at work, as you introduce yourself around, and in the social settings and one-on-one coffee "dates" I'm going to ask you to participate in. You can roll it out to break the ice.

You should gauge how much to reveal based on the corporate culture. If it's an old-school corporate setting, your script can be very narrow and tight. You can be more expansive if you're in a touchy-feely place.

The main thing is that your script should be authentic. It should be infused with your own special spice and your brand. People think they know an awful lot about me because of my script, the way I tell my story. It's not artificial or superficial, but I have been selective about what stories I tell. I talk about my adoption, my godchildren, my friendships, and dividing my time between Charlotte, North Carolina, and Hanover, New Hampshire. People know about my spirituality but not what my religion is. These things come from the real me—I'm not pulling my script from the sky. This is part of my persona, my history, the part I want my colleagues to know.

Here are some major points as you build your script:

Show you're a team player. Say something about why you wanted to work for the company, how delighted you are to be on this team, and how excited you are about what you can contribute. If you're junior, indicate that you're enthusiastic about learning, stretching, and contributing.

Give up something about yourself. Mention where you're from. Offer up one good childhood story that shows how you got your perseverance, your strength, your integrity, and values. Maybe you had to take care of your brothers and sisters growing up, which taught you leadership. Or perhaps your experience as a high school soccer player schooled you in group dynamics.

Talk about your life outside work. Share how you like jazz, reading, baseball, or throwing dinner parties. Mention a vacation you enjoyed. A child-related story is always safe, even if you don't have any—how about godchildren, nieces, and nephews? Dog stories work, too—I have won over many people with tales of Belle, my dog.

Rehearse your script. Try it out with friends and in front of the mirror. Get feedback from your "kitchen cabinet," your informal posse of mentors, peers, and allies—people who'll tell you the truth. Make sure you're comfortable with your script and that it sounds authentic.

There are some things you don't need to say. Here's what not to put in your script: "This is how [fill in the race or ethnicity] women do things." Pity stories aren't in your script. Guilt isn't in your script; people will totally shut down. Don't have a script that incites conflict or anger. Your script isn't "Here's what's wrong with the company." You shouldn't have an egomaniacal script: "Here's how much better I am than everybody else." Don't have a know-it-all script: "I know that already." Honest feedback from people you trust will help you avoid these traps.

Part of your script can be nonverbal. People get clues about who you are from how you decorate your office. Think about the corporate culture—do other people have a lot of personal items? If they have photographs of their husband or partner, children, and dogs, then you should, too. If they don't, you don't. And be careful not to put out anything that you don't feel comfortable talking about. Display some books—hot topics in management and leadership, for example. If you're more senior and have an office, how about some artwork? Ethnic art is fine, but don't get carried away. Just be prepared to talk about it. You can also be strategic. I know one woman who hung up all of her invitations to White House dinners along with different awards she had received. So when people meet with her, this is the backdrop that reminds them of who she is.

PLAN AN EARLY "WIN"

Come up with a project, assignment, contribution, or goal with bells and whistles that you can deliver on time. Show early on that you can shine. You don't have to accomplish the win in the first three months, but this is the time to figure out what it might be and formulate a plan.

Make sure your project aligns with the company's goals. To do that, you must know what they are. Tap into your networks and work your relationships for help and clarification. Your allies can also explain what constitutes a win in your particular organization. In some companies a win is an individual accomplishment; in others it's about leading a team. Be sure that you know what's important in your company's particular culture.

Do external research. See what your competitors are doing. Explore some of the more innovative, creative things that your competition is doing and tweak them for your company. Your team should help you do this. Don't go so far out of the box that it wouldn't fit in your organization. But is there something another company is doing that yours isn't? That research—being current and informed about the competition—also makes you look good.

Be clear that your win matters to your boss. Enough said.

Organize your troops. Make sure your team understands the goal and is on board. Within your group, you need some scouts. Their goal is to circulate (without revealing your plan) and bring back information. They are the ambassadors. It might be as simple as finding out who uses the conference room when, or as complex as knowing whom you need to collaborate with to get what you want.

Don't take on too much. It's easy to be too ambitious, especially in the first ninety days, and the results can be ruinous. So identify an opportunity that you can manage and deliver well and on time. If, after you've done the research, you realize that you've aimed too high or gone too large, scale back.

Tap into your strengths and how you can use them. This is the best, most efficient way to quickly make an impact.

Document your accomplishments. It's never too early to start documenting job successes. When it's time for your performance review, you want to be able to cite good things you've done throughout the year, including those achieved in the first ninety days.

First Ninety Days: The Essentials

- *Figure out the lay of the land quickly. In the first three months, watch and listen.*
- *Think strategically. Putting your nose to the grindstone is critical. But getting ahead (and even just staying afloat) takes more than hard work. You must come up with a game plan that includes your goals. You'll create it during these first ninety days.*
- *Unravel the company culture, both formal and informal. This will help you understand how you fit into the corporate community and how to maneuver.*
- *Write your observations down. Keep a journal, and include how you're feeling, your mistakes, and your victories.*
- *Shape and control your reputation or brand. It's better to define yourself than to allow yourself to be defined by other people. It will also help you sidestep stereotypes that still lurk in the workplace about women.*
- *Establish relationships with people all over the company. It's important to be a "social animal" when you first start a job. So schedule meetings and coffee or gym dates as often as you can.*
- *Get to know your team, including your manager. Team members can guide you as you find your way, can make you look good, and can help you succeed.*

What's Next?

Remember, the first ninety days is a time of flying low on the radar, not high. Your goal is to get the lay of the land and how you fit into it. You want to be visible, while also understanding where to be seen and where not to be seen.

At the end of the ninety days you need to have come up with a solid work plan. It must contain your goals and objectives, but it also has to have some action. It's definitely time for your "win." Your plan should have clear action steps as well as tasks and responsibilities you can delegate. It should also have outcomes and ways to monitor and measure them.

People at all levels, inside and outside the company, will help you achieve your big win and other goals. In the next chapter, I'll discuss in much more detail the kinds of relationships you must create and nurture in the new corporate landscape.

Chapter 5

Relationships: Cultivating Meaningful Connections

Recently, a former student of mine landed a job at a major international investment bank. I talked to her about getting to know the right people at work, and warned her that sometimes the key people aren't obvious. "You have to watch and learn and listen," I told her.

It turns out that in her area, there's a woman who works for an important manager. She doesn't appear high up on the organizational chart, but she's the woman to know. You might think it's more important to impress the top dog, not an administrator, but she's a gatekeeper. She controls the resources, and with a nod, she decides who stays and who goes. This woman has been at the company *forever*, though she's not socially friendly. You can't win her over; you have to prove yourself. Though she doesn't have the salary or title or corner office of a top manager, she runs that group. The bottom line is that the boys listen to her.

Cultivating relationships is the most important but most overlooked secret to career development and advancement. How well you perform is critically important to getting ahead. In fact, women, especially women of color, are expected to outperform our male peers in order to move forward. However, no one advances on performance alone; you also have to have good relationships. You have to take the time to make and nurture relationships with all kinds of people in your company and also maintain professional relationships outside your workplace. And the higher you climb the more significant these relationships become.

For many of us, relationship building is hard. Although we see others having coffee with senior managers, schmoozing after hours or on weekends, and working the room at the holiday party, we've been led to believe that all you have to do is work, work, work and that's enough. Many of us come in early, stay late, hole up at our desks, and work our tails off. That's good, but not good enough. We don't take the time to develop relationships with colleagues, peers, and managers, including those in the upper echelons. We're not talking to them; maybe we're not even looking up and smiling in the elevator or when we pass them in the hall. We're skipping the social events where we could meet and greet. We don't know those people, and worse, they don't know us.

The consequences are rough. Your managers and other upper-ups must have a sense of who you are and whether they can trust you before they offer you the kinds of assignments that give you visibility, hone your skills, and allow you to show off all that you know so that you can catapult to the top.

If you're a woman, building strong relationships isn't an option; *it's a must*. Even in this day and age, most of the powerful people are still male. And a lot of men don't truly understand women. When it comes to women of color, most didn't grow up with us or go to school with us. For some, all they know is what they've read in books or newspapers or seen on television or in the movies.

So building a relationship with them so that they can see you from an authentic perspective—beyond race, gender, and class—requires work on your part. You can't just assume it's going to happen. These guys aren't knocking down the door to get to know you. Instead of thinking, "I don't need to know anybody; I just need to show how hard I can work and how competent I am," you need to do the work *and* get yourself known.

Finally, as my former student learned—and I learned when I first began at Tuck—you can't afford to know just the senior people in your area. In the new workplace, you have to be able to work on a team, move around, transcend corporate borders, and cross over into different areas. You must build relationships all over your company and create a buzz for yourself that moves beyond your immediate specialty. Your relationships have to include all of the power players, not just the obvious ones.

In the last chapter, I discussed key relationships that you must create in the first ninety days. Here, I will explain in more detail how to grow and solidify relationships of all kinds.

THE WHO'S WHO AND WHAT'S WHAT OF WORKPLACE RELATIONSHIPS

Your allies, mentors, sponsors, and professional connections in your network are people who are on your side and have your back. They help you learn, advance, and grow. It's important to know that the old rules about networking and finding a mentor to get ahead don't apply. You can't just get hooked up with the mentor your company provides and expect to get ahead. And networking is much more than collecting business cards. These days you need a sponsor—someone high up in the company who can take you under his or her wing, and offer visibility, protection, and a boost upward. The truth is, each of these relationships is important.

Mentors: The Personal Meets the Professional

Mentors come in all shapes and sizes. A mentor has to be somebody you trust, who can help you by offering information and advice specific to you and your career as you develop and grow. You can have mentors inside and outside of your company, and they can serve as both role models and friends.

Mentors don't have to be on the high end of the food chain. If that's the only place you're looking, you've got the wrong approach. Everybody has something to offer. My dean at Tuck is a wonderful mentor. We can sit down and bat an idea back and forth, sometimes in a gracious way, sometimes with a bit more of an edge. I can go to him when times are tough and also when I've got accomplishments to celebrate. Some of the things he says hurt my feelings. But they also may help me stretch and grow. After talking to him, I always come up in a better place, with a better product.

But he's not my only mentor. The audiovisual staff also mentors me. I'm not the most technical person, but I have to do video and PowerPoint presentations in my classes. Thank the Lord for the AV guys. They help me look good by making sure my presentations are excellent. They show me the latest stuff, teach me how to use the newest machine, and look into what else is out there. They have knowledge and experience that I don't have and they're kind enough to share it. Remember, mentors can be on any level or play a variety of roles. Think of it as having a constellation of support around you.

Most companies assign you a mentor when you're first starting out. That person helps you understand how things work and find your way through the system and culture. However, as we've said, you can—and should—have more than one. To find mentors, you'll need to do some homework, scout the horizon, and figure out who can help you get to where you want to go. It sometimes takes time, patience, and resilience to build a full-fledged mentoring relationship. But you can do it if you're honest, authentic, assertive, and real. (For tips on how to strike up a conversation with a possible mentor, see the sidebar "Mastering the Elevator Speech.")

One last thing to remember about mentors: it's not just about what they can do for you. At the end of the year, I give each member of the AV team a bottle of wine. Mentorship should always be about giving to each other.

Lift As You Climb: Successful Mentoring

Shawna Wilson and Cindi Lee Evans both work for PepsiCo in Texas. Shawna is Cindi's mentor, and they have a unique and wonderful relationship. Here, each of them—mentor and mentee—talk about their bond.

Cindi's Story

I have never shied away from hard work. I started babysitting in eighth grade and worked all through high school. At the University of Houston, I was a double major and paid my way through school, working two jobs, one full-time and the other part-time. It was a lot, but I have a big family. I needed to take responsibility for my education and also help my parents out.

I graduated in 2002 and joined Frito-Lay, part of PepsiCo, in Dallas. After a year I was managing fourteen employees and twenty-six stores where our products were sold. At one of the company's rollout meetings, I got selected to give a speech to motivate the team. That speech gave me exposure to everyone at the meeting, including Shawna Wilson.

When a position opened up in Houston, where she was based, Shawna remembered my speech and interviewed me. During that interview she talked about her background, and I talked about mine. We realized that we had so much in common and really hit it off. I didn't end up in that job; instead I found a mentor.

I had been assigned a mentor by the company, so at first my relationship with Shawna was informal. But after six months we decided to make it official. As we grew closer and she shared her advice and wisdom, one of the things I mentioned to Shawna was that I considering going to business school. I'll be honest. The University of Houston is a commuter school. I went there because I could afford it. So when I was thinking about business schools, I set an attainable goal—the University of Texas at Dallas.

But Shawna was very clear that I should aim higher. Her idea was that I should consider leaving my job to attend a big-time business school full-time.

I try to be realistic, and at the time, this Ivy League idea didn't feel that way. How was I going to get in? My undergraduate grades weren't great. I still had school loans, so I didn't even know how I was going to pay the $1,000 for the Princeton Review to prepare for the GMAT! But after I told Shawna these things, she continued to encourage me to aim high. Then she wrote out a $1,000 check to pay for the review course. I was so surprised and grateful. I had never seen anybody do something like this for someone else unless they were related.

I am going to business school, and it's because of Shawna. She's the reason I am where I am. She's motivated me, taught me not to limit my possibilities, and broadened my ideas about how far I can go. And she doesn't just say it; she takes action. She shows that she believes in me.

As I move ahead with my life, I owe it to myself to do well and make the most of my opportunities. But I also owe it to Shawna. She's been a blessing, and I fully intend to make sure she always understands what a big impact she has had. And, too, the buck doesn't stop with me. I have promised myself that I will "pay it forward" and be a mentor—like Shawna is to me—for someone else.

Shawna's Story

When I first met Cindi, right away I thought, *Gosh, that's a smart girl. What an up-and-comer.* And after I interviewed her for a position, I was really floored. Sitting down with her, I was impressed with how well she carried herself. She was accomplished, and also sweet, easy to like. I could see that she was a shining star in the making. As I sat with her, I saw myself.

After that first meeting, I became an informal mentor to her, but also a sponsor. Behind the scenes, I began to push to get her out of her entry-level role, to a place where she could shine. Eventually she was promoted from district sales manager to zone business manager. A zone is a $100 million business, up from the $9.5 million that she managed before.

At one point, Cindi became frustrated with her job. Because I knew what was being said behind closed doors, I told her, "Don't walk out the door. There are lots of people who are your supporters, but you might have to be patient." Eventually things smoothed out, and in 2007 she got the offer she wanted.

As our mentor-mentee relationship progressed, we talked about the idea of Cindi getting an MBA. She mentioned SMU and UT Dallas. But I pushed her: "Have you thought about a big name? Harvard? Wharton? Kellogg? Tuck?" First she looked at me like I had four heads. Then she said, "Listen, I wasn't that great a student, and I really don't come from a rich family. There's no way I can get in." I looked Cindi in the eye and said, "I'm just like you. I didn't come from a rich family, either." I pulled out my transcript from college and said, "See, I didn't walk out of Ohio State with a 4.0, but I got into Kellogg." And then I told her, "I believe in you so much that I'm giving you this." I wrote out a check for $1,000 for the *Princeton Review*. I told her that I didn't want the money back, and she didn't have to go, but I wanted her to think bigger and to simply try.

I understood where she was coming from. When I first started thinking about my own MBA, I was working in California and looking at Cal State. But somebody took me under his wing and said, "Think bigger," so I ended up at Kellogg. I wanted to do the same for Cindi, especially knowing that no one around her was telling her to aim that high.

I began trying to get her to different Frito-Lay events to meet people, directors and managing directors, who would get her to think bigger. My advice was, "Don't be intimidated. You're as good as everyone else." You know what? Cindi got a 650 on her GMAT, and we began talking about Tuck.

I've been at PepsiCo for eighteen years and was lucky to have some people who mentored me along the way. Cindi isn't the first person I've mentored, but she has the most potential. Mentoring is a responsibility of mine, a way to give back. And it's also very rewarding for me to see Cindi reach and grow, learn and shine.

SPONSORS: A HELPING HAND FROM HIGH

A sponsor is a powerful person in your organization who uses his or her social capital to help you advance. A sponsor stands behind you, attaches his or her name to you, and provides connections, visibility, exposure, and coaching. Sponsors also offer protection. In tough economic times, however, people get left behind, and your sponsor may not be able to protect you. Sometimes they can't even protect themselves. But what I've seen sponsors do, even if they themselves have been caught up in layoffs and reassignments, is take people with them. If, God forbid, you do lose your job, a sponsor can also offer references and connections to help you find another position.

What a sponsor isn't? Your best friend. Sponsorship is generally a professional relationship. A sponsor doesn't have to have a deep relationship with you. He or she needs just enough information to be willing to take a chance on you. An executive may sponsor you and you may never know who he or she is. It's the conversation about you that goes on behind closed doors. You don't know who's in that room. But when your name comes up, your sponsor's the one who vouches for you, or at minimum has enough confidence in you to say, "Let's give her a shot."

How do you find a sponsor? You've hit the jackpot if someone from the executive suite picks you to sponsor. But that may not happen. As with finding a mentor, you may have to think strategically and seek out someone who can sponsor you. For help approaching a potential sponsor, start with an elevator speech.

MASTERING THE ELEVATOR SPEECH

I've seen the most confident, extraordinary women freeze up at company events. They walk in, see all these senior white men, and freeze. They have no idea what to say. It can be even worse face-to-face.

In the previous chapter, I discussed the importance of developing a script to help you shape your brand. Now I'd like you to prepare an elevator speech so you know what to say when you bump into a senior manager. It's not just for the elevator. It's a script that highlights a few important things about you, shows that you're interested and engaged in the company, and demonstrates that you both are confident and have respect for the person you're talking to. It's a very spiffy, tight paragraph not only showing who you are but also offering insight into your curiosity and wisdom. It shows that you're a contributor with specific ideas.

Women often shy away from these conversations. It feels false, like brown-nosing or sucking up. We assume that because we are working hard and have all these great ideas, people automatically have heard about them.

But in reality they most likely don't know. They need you to talk to them. You'd better believe your male colleagues are doing that. But we've got to get much better at it.

You can lean on your speech at company events or when approaching—or running into—one of the upper-ups, particularly if you're interested in being mentored or sponsored by that person. An elevator speech requires research and forward thinking.

Before you get started, do your best to relax and be as authentic and natural as you can. Then your speech might go like this:

1. Introduce yourself.
2. Say something flattering: "You're one of my role models," or "I've long admired your work."
3. Be specific: "I understand you're working on such and such, and it's very impressive. Tell me more about that."
4. Now say something about you that shows you're a strategic thinker: "I'm working on such-and-such, and here's what I'm thinking. I've learned this and that and believe we could apply it to what you're working on," or "I just read an article about one of our competitors' projects. If we tweak it this way, here's what it might look like for us."
5. If your conversation is more formal—a coffee or lunch date—follow up with a handwritten note on good stationery. Take a few minutes to say thank you and why talking to the person was important to you. As an ending, say, "Hope we get a chance to connect again." When people get a note card, they think, *Wow*, especially in the age of digital communication. That signals something special about you, that you are gracious. With email, you press the delete key and it's gone. The note card goes on the desk, a constant reminder of who you are.

Remember to keep it upbeat. Your conversation is about showing people you're confident, you have a presence, and you can play in the same sandbox as the big guys. Be sure to practice so you'll be ready to take advantage of the opportune moments—in the elevator or anywhere.

ALLIES: SUPPORTERS IN THE WORKPLACE

Webster's defines an ally as a person who cooperates with another person; a supporter or comrade. At work, allies are the collection of people who help each other. They support you when times are tough and celebrate with you when all's good. Having allies in different parts of the company is essential. If you're preparing a presentation on a new product, your friend in R & D can give you the back story, while your ally in marketing can help make your visuals extra snazzy.

Allies in the workplace can be men or women, and it's important to have both, but here I'd like to focus on the critical value of having female allies. Research has shown that women can be their own worst enemies at work, unlike men. Too often, we don't seek each other out as allies. The situation gets even worse across race and culture lines.

Allies do four things:

1. They give you a sense that you are not alone.
2. They help you strategize everything from your next project to another position. For instance, when putting together a presentation, you can call an ally in finance to help with the numbers.
3. They offer constructive feedback. They can point out things you might not be doing or doing well while still being on your side.
4. They provide access to information. They can explain what's happening in the informal network, give you the scoop about restructuring or cost cutting, or alert you to a new opportunity that might be coming up soon in another area.

While men are connecting on the golf course or after work

over a Scotch, women shy away from making connections with each other. Some women don't believe that other women can help them. Others are mired in individualism—that there can be only one female star. For others, it feels too "girly."

However, building alliances with other women is beneficial and rewarding. As women, we must look out for each other. We must help other women develop and pull them to the table when we can. How do you reach out to another woman? Be authentic. Have the courage to take the time to connect with another woman. Get to know her. And keep in mind that these alliances are about career building, not about snagging another girlfriend. Don't confuse your female work ally with "your girl." It's okay to share some personal information, but in general, keep the conversations professional.

THE NETWORK: THE PEOPLE WHO CREATE YOUR BUZZ

Your network is made up of the people of all levels inside your company and outside it who provide information, advice, and support. Your network helps create good buzz about you—passing the word that you're a team player, are capable, have a curious mind, and possess all the other attributes that are part of the brand you want to nurture.

Don't forget the support people, like the gatekeeper at my former student's company and my AV guys. It's important to develop those relationships. These people know how to get on people's calendars, offer protection, and make you look good. So get to know and appreciate them. It's always the simple, gracious things that count: bring coffee to your receptionist, or when you buy flowers for your desk, get some for your assistant, too.

As you build a network around you, think about what professional organizations you should belong to. When companies are looking to hire new people, they look to professional groups for advice and guidance. Professional associations of all sorts help you learn what's hot in your industry and meet movers and shakers or at least get to listen to them at workshops and conferences. It's easy to research groups online; also, ask your peers and colleagues for suggestions. Often your company will cover the cost to attend.

Alumni associations are also very important. Just because you've finished school doesn't mean you're finished with the school! And don't forget social networking websites such as Linked In.com or those specific to your field, such as Mediabistro.com for publishing. Turn back to chapter 3 for more information.

Finally, take the time to give back to your network. It shouldn't be all about you. Have coffee with a young college alum who asks for your advice, volunteer for a committee, help plan a national conference, conduct a workshop, or mentor a student. You don't have to do everything, but be active and authentic.

TOUGH TALKS

Some relationships are simply difficult. In a large workplace full of complex, diverse personalities, you can't get along with everyone. What's the key to managing difficult relationships and the challenging conversations that come with them? My friend Dr. Bernardo M. Ferdman says he relies on compassion. "It isn't about kumbaya and holding hands," he says. "It's about being a 'diplomatic warrior' and finding ways to effectively, authentically, and productively manage conflict as you move toward a collective goal."

Dr. Ferdman is a professor at the Marshall Goldsmith

School of Management at Alliant International University in San Diego and a very thoughtful man who studies diversity, inclusion, and conflict management. Here, I asked him to offer some advice and resources for dealing with the conflicts that arise at work:

1. Take a step back. Look at the situation thoughtfully, beyond (but without excluding) the emotions. What are you trying to address with a particular relationship or interaction? Until you address the issue, you can't solve it. Think about what you want. What would be a positive outcome? Are you disagreeing about some specific thing that happened? Is it a pattern or the process that's the issue? Is it a style?

2. Be honest. Rather than heaping all the blame on the other person, see your own role. Look in the mirror and ask yourself to be vulnerable. Understand yourself in the picture. What could you do—if you weren't so angry—to move toward the other person's position? What have you contributed to the interaction?

3. Take the high road. Imagine the other person as good instead of evil. Try to see his or her point of view and emotions. That opens up the possibility that you might understand (or seek to understand) the person's motivation. You aren't excusing anybody, but creating a space, a safe place for a conversation.

4. Make the first move. Break the "silence spiral" by reaching out.

5. It's helpful to discuss what you're feeling—but without being *in* the emotions. Tell the other person about your anger and frustration, but don't blow up in the middle of the conversation. Keep in mind that feel-

ings are complex. You can have mixed feelings, like anger and appreciation, at the same time. Say things like, "This is what I'm feeling—what about you? I'd like to have a positive working relationship. What about you?"

6. Create solutions. In most cases, you have a common goal—getting the work done. So open your mind and heart to brainstorm and engage in a learning conversation. Ask questions and generate new ideas. Approach from the spirit of dialogue, not from the perspective of "I'm right."

7. Finally, don't forget that there are different ways to handle conflict. It's important to have an expanded repertoire. Sometimes a learning conversation is appropriate, sometimes not. (A learning conversation is focused on understanding and listening, rather than being right or getting your way.) In some cases, avoiding the issue may be your best way to cope, particularly if it's not a big deal. Sometimes give in; other times be constructive but try to get your way. Use your instinct and emotional intelligence to figure out what's best.

For further reading on managing difficult relationships, Dr. Ferdman suggests these books:

Crucial Confrontations: Tools for Talking About Broken Promises, Violated Expectations, and Bad Behavior (McGraw-Hill), by Kerry Patterson, Joseph Grenny, Ron McMillan, and Al Switzler

Crucial Conversations: Tools for Talking When Stakes Are High (McGraw-Hill), by Kerry Patterson, Joseph Grenny, Ron McMillan, and Al Switzler

Difficult Conversations: How to Discuss What Matters Most (Penguin), by Douglas Stone, Bruce Patton, Sheila Heen, and Roger Fisher

Discussing the Undiscussable: A Guide to Overcoming Defensive Routines in the Workplace (Jossey-Bass Business and Management), by William R. Noonan

THE IMPORTANCE OF SOCIALIZING

I'm often asked, "Do I have to play golf? Do I have to go to the holiday party? Do I have to join the company softball team?"

The answer to each of these questions is no. Of course you don't *have* to. You can succeed without playing golf, you can advance without going to the holiday party, and people get ahead without spending Friday nights drinking or playing ball with the work crew.

Still, the reality is you have to find ways to fraternize with your colleagues. As the line between our work and home lives has blurred and teamwork has become an extremely valued attribute, you must engage in informal activities with the people with whom you work. The higher up you go in an organization, the more people socialize and fraternize. By hanging out with your colleagues, people get to see you informally, you expand your network, and people get more comfortable with you—and you with them.

Some people are better at socializing than others. I've seen people who are confident, can work a room, and are great self-promoters—and they use these skills to hide weak performance. At the other extreme, there are those who work like dogs, but nobody ever sees them because they're more comfortable hunched over their desk than they are working the room at a cocktail party. The secret is that you need *both* performance and presence. It's not one or the other.

So if you're a strong performer but your social skills are a little weak, pick your poison. You don't want to take golf lessons? Then be prepared to show up at the summer outing. It's the easiest of the poisons to swallow.

Here's your party strategy:

- Get a nice, appropriate outfit, festive but not overdone. This is an office holiday party; you aren't going to a club. Don't overdo the makeup.
- Arrive early; don't go in there late.
- Head to the bar and order a wine spritzer, wine mixed with seltzer. A work event isn't the time to explore new cocktails. That one drink should last you all night long.
- Be strategic. Look around the room and figure out who's who. Who's there from the executive suite? Whom do you need to introduce yourself to? Whom do you need to say "season's greetings" to? If you're uncomfortable, go in with a script and rehearse it ahead of time. Mention something you're planning to do over the holidays. Say something from your elevator speech.
- About forty minutes after you've connected with a few people, you can get your coat and go. Better yet, plan to meet up with some girlfriends and go somewhere fun. Think of it as your "festivities night," with the office party as your first stop.
- Don't drag along a date unless you're in a committed relationship. And never bring a different date to each party!
- Companies have other outlets beyond the holiday party.

Indeed, in tough economic times there may be no end-of-the-year celebration at all. Get the lay of the land. Does your company have a sports team you can join? A company picnic? Is it connected to a philanthropic or volunteer organization? You don't have to do everything. Pick and choose, but you have to go to a few, and you have to connect with people on an informal, non-work-related basis.

You can also bring your colleagues to you. If you're competing in a race or community sports tournament, invite people to cheer you on. If you sing in the choir, invite people to church when you're singing. I know someone who did that. It was a huge learning experience for the people she worked with. My coauthor has a friend who is a high-level publishing executive by day, opera singer by night. When she invited her colleagues to hear her sing, everyone was stunned and amazed. Her profile at work shot up.

And, by the way, if you really are thinking about getting ahead, learn how to play golf. More and more women are playing—and it's fun.

Guess Who's *Not* Coming to Dinner?

At one of the companies I consult for, I worked with a woman who had a difficult experience negotiating an informal relationship with her supervisor. I'd like to share this story to illustrate the value of making this kind of relationship work—even when it's extremely tricky.

––––––––

The woman I was coaching was clearly on the fast track. She had received several very challenging assignments with tough managers to get her ready for bigger things. In one assignment in a small work group, she was the youngest person, the only person of color, and the only one who was single. She had been excited and prided herself on having good relationships . . . until this work group.

Her manager and his wife had a passion for doing dinner parties. Once a month, they would invite someone from the work group—along with his or her spouse—to their home for an extravagant meal. That employee would then report back on what the boss and his wife had served and how wonderful it all was. After months of this, it created a ripple effect of excitement and anticipation.

The woman I was coaching was waiting eagerly for her invitation. But after everyone in the entire group had eaten at the boss's house, she realized that her invitation wasn't coming. The other work group members would talk about the meal and how great it tasted, but they'd have the conversation around her as though she wasn't there. As she became more and more invisible, she felt increasingly isolated and vulnerable. The voice inside her head started first whispering, then shouting, *Why can't he see me? I'm being excluded and everybody knows it. I'm really pissed off. I'm going to go in there and tell him off.*

By the time she started working with me, she had decided to demand a transfer. Instead, I suggested she take the lead and invite her boss and his wife to dinner. She said, "No way! I don't want them in my house. I don't want them to see where I live. Why should I cook for them? I'm not their maid!"

Okay, plan B. I suggested she go to his office and frame it this way: "I know everybody's been invited to dinner, but I haven't. I'd love to get to know you on an informal level and also meet your wife. I'd like to invite you to my favorite restaurant for dinner—my treat. I know you've cooked great meals; this restaurant has a great chef. When can we go?" I reminded her not to be angry and to keep it light. If he said no, then it'd be time for her to get out of the group.

When she went in, the man was flabbergasted. She had boxed him into a corner. He didn't say no; he accepted.

The point of this story? Socializing at work can be difficult and even strange. But it's part of the landscape, so sometimes you have to be the bigger person. Maybe what the boss did wasn't intentional. Perhaps he wasn't comfortable bringing home a single woman. Who knows? I always advise being direct, rather than angry and hostile. Try something like "I'm just trying to understand, because I want to be part of the team, too. But this is making me uncomfortable." Then if you don't see a change, it really is time to move up and out. Or perhaps it's time to think of better ways of managing up, down, and across your organization.

MANAGING UP, DOWN, AND ACROSS

Entire books have been written about how to manage people. I can't tell you everything you need to know—and part of your success will depend on your emotional intelligence, patience, open-mindedness, and grace. To discuss managing relationships, I consulted a pro. Dr. Stacy Blake-Beard is an associate professor of management at the Simmons School of Management in Boston and a member of the research faculty at the Center for Gender in Organizations. "The best relationships are mutually beneficial," says Dr. Blake-Beard. "And they're also genuine. People have a barometer for authenticity. When you show up or arrive in a way that isn't real, that lack of authenticity gets in the way of beneficial relationships."

Here, with the help of Dr. Blake-Beard, I'd like to offer you some big-picture thoughts that most people forget when managing up, down, and across.

Managing Up: Your Boss Isn't the Boss of You

When thinking about the boss, most of us need to be reminded that he or she is dependent on you. Too many people cede control to their managers way too often. The way you work together should be based on interdependence, rather than hierarchy. Nobody can do his or her job in isolation—especially these days when teamwork is so highly valued. Your boss needs you in order to shine.

So how do you get your manager to work for you? Know what your boss needs. What are his or her deadlines, timelines, and goals? When you figure out, very specifically, how to support your manager, you both succeed.

Managing Further Up: Get to Know Your Boss's Boss

Managing up shouldn't stop at your direct manager. You should have a relationship with your boss's boss. He or she might be the best person to explain to you what the game plan for the company is and how can you contribute to that. He or she should also know who you are and what you're thinking.

An easy way is to send an email. Always let your manager know that you are doing this so he or she doesn't feel that you're sneaking around. Request a coffee date—ten or fifteen minutes—to check in. Ask questions such as, "How would you define leadership here? How do you see the big picture at the company? To what should we be paying attention? What's your game plan for getting us to that place?" Of course, you have to do your research before a meeting like this. Send a note—not an email—to say thank you.

By the way, this kind of sit-down is appropriate only at companies where the culture isn't highly bureaucratic, hierarchical, or authoritarian. If it is, then connecting with the upper-ups at social or cultural events may be the better move.

When you do meet with your manager's manager, steer clear of talking about your manager. Your job is to make your manager look good and to contribute to the success of the team and the company as a whole.

Managing "Down": It's About Leadership with a Personal Touch

The ability to inspire others to join you on the journey you're on is an art. And it's not a skill reserved for those in the executive suite. Leadership is critical at every level and in every area.

Like managing up, leadership is two-way. And it's hard work. How do you motivate other people to sign on to your vision? You have to know and understand the people you're leading as individuals, since what might inspire employee A won't necessarily work for employee B. These individual differences mean that as a leader, you need to be thoughtful, attentive, in contact, and in touch—not just in charge.

Managing Across: Your Sanity Check

Most of us spend so much time thinking about our bosses or direct reports that we neglect our peers. But peers can be a huge source of support in your career. They can provide you with important data about the company, particularly parts that you aren't as familiar with. They can also offer information about the people above and below you—and give you insight into your own brand and buzz. Peers also offer a fairly safe sounding board and, in the best-case scenario, can offer honest, informed feedback. Think of them as your sanity check.

TALK THE SMALL TALK

Your colleagues can make you or break you. No matter what, they need to see you as part of the team. This doesn't mean you have to go out every Friday drinking with them. But you do need to have a conversation with them. My good friend Carla Harris uses this approach. If all the guys talk sports on Monday and you know diddly-bop about football, at least watch the eleven o'clock news or read the sports section so you can have a conversation about who won and maybe make one intelligent observation about the team or the game.

If sports isn't your thing—or even theirs—figure out a few icebreakers. As I've mentioned elsewhere, children are a safe topic, even if you don't have any. I talk about my godchildren and nieces and nephews with my colleagues. And my dog. Everyone knows Belle. A picture of your pooch in your office can spark a conversation or even an ongoing dialogue. Cooking, music, and travel are other safe bets. Don't pick topics that are too controversial. Generally, stay away from religion and politics.

A FEW FINAL THOUGHTS ON RELATIONSHIP BUILDING

If you're serious about developing and advancing your career, you have to be able to build relationships. You have to have conversations with your coworkers. You don't need to love the people you work with, but you do need to respect them and have them respect you. You need to show empathy and compassion and be able to receive it. You should be able to trust people, although not necessarily everybody. And no matter how strong your relationships at every level, you still need to perform your tail off. You will still have to prove yourself . . . every day.

Still, there's a limit to what relationships can accomplish and how long and hard you should work at creating and leveraging connections at a company. If your stomach turns over twice going in the front door, maybe you don't need to be there. If you're sitting in your office feeling angry, isolated, and bitter and thinking that you'll never succeed, think twice. If you don't respect the people and their values and belief systems or if you just don't like them, you don't need to be there. If you don't see yourself advancing, developing, growing, or flourishing, you don't need to be there.

On the other hand, you do have to look for the light in the darkness. Seek out those people who are going to give you the support, nurturing, and feedback to help you be successful. They are there; but you have to seek them out. Look for the lights in the darkness. Who's educable? Whom can you bring over to your side?

As you make these meaningful connections, it's important not to be exploitive and manipulative. That mentality doesn't serve well. Remember, relationships follow you from company to company. You might not work with the same people, but the connections you make add up to a powerful learning and support network for you. Make sure these are renewable relationships.

Relationships: The Essentials

- *Building relationships at work may be hard, especially if you're shy. But creating and nurturing strong, authentic relationships—with people at every level—can make or break your career.*
- *Get mentored. A mentor can offer you information, advice, and guidance. Your company may assign you a mentor when you first start out. But you can also have more than one.*
- *Find a sponsor—or, better, let one find you. A sponsor is someone high up in your company who can help you get ahead.*
- *Design an elevator speech. This is a thoughtful paragraph you can pull out in the elevator or anywhere else when speaking to upper management. It should show that you're excited to be at the company and have something to contribute.*
- *Cultivate allies. This is your support team inside the organization.*
- *Build a network. These are people of all levels, inside the company and outside it, that offer information, advice, and guidance. Tap former colleagues, professional and alumni groups, and online social networks.*
- *Don't skip parties and other workplace social settings. Face time is critical, and the higher up you go, the more people socialize together.*
- *Give back. Relationships at every level should be two-way, not only all about you.*

What's Next?

Now that you understand the importance relationships and of smart, thoughtful communication, you'll take those skills with you to your performance review. Chapter 6 will explain why a review is so important, how to prepare for an effective review, how to be evaluated fairly, and also how to conduct one.

Job Performance:
It's Not the Only Thing,
but It Is the Main Thing

Performance is critical. You can't just "do it"; you've got to do it well. Nobody wants a regular Joe; they want a star. You also have to be able to *show* that your performance is above and beyond the call of duty, especially if you're a woman. People in your company—your manager and the upper-ups in the executive suite—need to understand what you're bringing to the table. You must be able to demonstrate that you can deliver a product, manage resources, meet your numbers, and develop your team efficiently and effectively. This is true more than ever in times of economic turmoil when companies are restructuring. Either you perform or you're out the door, as so many have found out.

Rating performance, however, can be very tricky. Reviews and evaluations are time-consuming and aren't always easy to either give or receive. These days, most companies have changed the way they assess an employee's work record. Back in the day, the evaluation was basically a one-page checklist that looked at attendance and quality of work; it was a simple scorecard, efficient and effective, that asked, "Did you do your job?"

But that's changed in the past decade. First, the standards are different. In the new fast-paced global economy that relies on knowledge and technology, the stakes are much higher than they used to be—and the ante goes up with your salary. Corporations now have fewer layers of management, so teamwork is critical. And rather than having one specific skill, like accounting or marketing, the most valuable employees have multiple "competencies." So you must be able to show that you have a broad set of abilities that can be applied across different areas of the company. Corporations also like multitaskers, employees with many skills who can work on and deliver more than one project at once. All of these changes affect how you are evaluated.

The performance evaluation itself has changed, too, again because of technology, globalization, and the changing corporate structure. As companies have reduced the layers of management and encouraged teamwork, you might have fewer managers over you, and you could be reporting to someone in a different state or even another country. This means that the onus of proving what you've accomplished is on you. Plus, technology creates an unbelievable "paper trail" of emails, which means that you must have a paper trail of your own.

Even before these kinds of changes made evaluating performance more complex, women frequently undervalued the importance of the review and looked at both giving and receiving reviews as a chore. But you must remember: the performance appraisal is a critical learning tool. It allows you to be proactive, to tell your own story, to make sure you're treated fairly and can move ahead—in status and salary. You can understand how your supervisor views you and your work, and it allows you to be clear about what's expected of you.

A performance review—and the groundwork leading up to it—is very useful in identifying, understanding, and leveraging your strengths and contributions. It's also an opportunity for you to detail the quality of your work, how you've succeeded, and where you need to stretch and grow. And finally, if you're laid off, a positive performance evaluation can help open the door to your next position.

Given what's at stake, you must learn to make your performance review work for you.

THE PERFORMANCE REVIEW SURVIVAL GUIDE

I asked two of my most trusted advisors and colleagues to provide some practical strategies for getting the most out of the review process. Dr. Stella Nkomo, professor of management at the University of South Africa's Graduate School of Business Leadership and coauthor of my first book, *Our Separate Ways*, and Dr. Laura Morgan Roberts, an assistant professor of organizational behavior at Harvard Business School, offer this advice.

Lay the groundwork. Most women (most men, too) skip the vital ingredient for getting a thorough and fair review: laying the groundwork. It's surprising how many employees have no idea that this is necessary and even less of a clue of how to do it. Here's the secret: at least a year before your first review—generally when you're first hired—you must find out what's expected of you, how success is measured, what your goals are, and what resources you'll have to accomplish them. You must get this clearly spelled out and agreed upon. This is your performance plan. It's also crucial that you find out how your boss defines excellence. Don't assume you know! And don't assume your manager is going to lay this out for you. You may have to draft your plan and then get him or her to approve it.

For instance, if you're responsible for a sales function, you need to know what your benchmark is. What's expected in terms of numbers for the next quarters? If you're in R & D, what's expected of you in the area of innovation? You, your supervisor, and the other members of the team must be clear about the targets, the time frame, and the metrics—how performance is measured.

Then, when your review rolls around, it'll be there in black and white. No drama, just the facts: *This is what we agreed that I would do, this is how I planned to do it, this is what I did, and here are the results.* Either you succeeded and got results or you didn't.

Of course, make sure you *are* performing! If you're more junior, you need to be clear that you're not doing anything to get in the way of either your team's or your manager's success. You must be meeting your deadlines, gathering the correct data, doing analysis in a crisp, clear way, bringing new ideas to the team, and communicating them clearly and coherently. Always consider ways to learn, grow, and stretch. Keep in mind where you want your career to go and the key assignments that will move you ahead.

If you're more senior, you should be setting the tone for your group and creating a vision for your team. Think big picture.

Be clear that the goals you set for yourself are valued by the organization. This is important to think about as you lay the groundwork.

In the past, the annual review compared what you did with the duties spelled out in your job description. But the era of the job description is over. The new business environment is dynamic, competitive, and volatile, which makes a job description too static. Most companies—something like 60 percent—use a balanced scorecard system to align business activities with the vision and strategy of the organization. In this process, your performance is tied to a giant scorecard that encompasses the company's own goals.

What exactly does this mean for you? You must make sure that what you do is in line with what your company wants to achieve in the next year. You have to be making a contribution to the broader goals of the organization, not just getting your job done.

Too often you may be working very hard, trying to prove yourself, and even feeling proud of your accomplishments. Yet what you're doing isn't valued or adding value.

First and foremost, you must know what the company's strategic plan is. This isn't deep: it's in your company's annual report and/or its website. Ask someone, a colleague or your manager. Then sit down with your manager and figure out the specific thing or things you're going to do to contribute to the broader picture, to the company's success. This is also a good discussion to have with your allies and mentors. These colleagues can help you and give you the information, clarification, and support that you need.

Document, document, document. In most cases, it's on you to prove that your performance has made a difference. Managers can't be expected to remember everything, and they tend to recall the extremes—extremely good, extremely poor. And research shows they remember the negative best! So during the year, keep track of everything you do—your results, your accomplishments, and your achievements. Be as specific as you can. Your journal will come in handy here. If you have documentation, you can sit down with your "evidence" and reach the conclusion that you did a really great job on building customer relations, for example.

Do a self-review first. In many cases, this is a requirement. The manager will put the ball in your court, so you should be ready. Think: if you had to rate yourself, how would you do it? Be as honest and specific as possible, offering concrete examples. Ask what new challenges you'd like to take on and what on-the-job accomplishments demonstrate that readiness. Practice what you're going to say, so that you feel confident and ready for your meeting with your manager.

Stay positive and confident. Walk into your review confident that you understand what you did well and that you can articulate your accomplishments, your challenges, and what you need to do to grow and improve. If you've done the preparation, you've performed to the best of your ability, and you know what the metrics are, you should be able to present a balanced, realistic picture of your year.

Be open to feedback. Your evaluation is two-way. You've got to be open for feedback. Don't walk in frowning with body language that says, *I don't care what you're saying, I'm not listening, and don't ask questions.* Take off the psychological armor. Uncross your arms, and definitely don't put your hands on your hips. Offer nonconfrontational eye contact. Be sure you're not wearing all black, and let your hair down. The person evaluating you is looking to see how you're handling the feedback and needs to know you're interested in growing. If you're too confrontational, it will spark defensiveness. Listen actively and take notes. You don't have to swallow everything you hear, but he or she may have nuggets of wisdom that could be useful for you. Don't take anything personally. Your attitude should be: *I'm in learning, growing, stretching mode and this review is part of the process.* Ask what else you can do to contribute, and say thank you as you leave. Besides, if you've done the work up front—you're clear about what's expected, you've performed well, and you have the documentation to prove it—this shouldn't be the worst conversation in the world. On the contrary, it should set you on your course for improving your performance in the future.

GETTING A FAIR REVIEW

Research shows that subtle, generally unconscious bias can get in the way of managers giving some employees a full, fair performance assessment. This is true for women, particularly women of color.

Understand that subtle race, gender, and cultural discrimination may be lurking in the room even before you sit down for your review. Studies have persistently identified the "think manager, think male" phenomenon. In essence, this means that men are viewed as better management material because they are thought to have more of the characteristics—male characteristics—that make good managers. Of course this isn't true, but it fosters bias against women in managerial selection, placement, promotion, training decisions . . . and reviews.

More subtly, managers may feel awkward rating employees who are different from them. This discomfort can be manifested in a few ways. To put it bluntly, white male managers, for instance, often hold back from giving their female employees of color frank feedback because they fear charges of discrimination. Or they've been told that the company has a diversity program and it's important to make women and employees of color feel good. So they don't tell the truth. Other times they're simply uncomfortable. I've actually heard a male manager say, "I never give low ratings to women because I'm afraid they'll cry. And I hate to see women cry!"

At the other end of the spectrum, some managers hold women, especially women of color, to a different standard. If you're in sales or finance, you may not be expected to succeed because of the stereotypes that women aren't aggressive or good at math. So even if you're walking on water, they don't believe it.

Either way, feedback that's not constructive won't help you reach your full potential. To combat this and other performance evaluation concerns, many companies are now using 360 reviews. Also called the multi-rater system, this is a full-circle process in which, along with a manager, peers, direct reports, and even clients provide input about an employee. Ideally, the views are aggregated and you get a summary of what the participants (generally five) think about your work. Though this technique has its flaws, it does help reduce the bias that one person may be harboring.

If your manager's feedback is too general, ask for specifics. Tell him or her that above all, your goal is to do an excellent job, and that you value his or her input in figuring out how to work smarter. Ask:

- What skills and competencies are expected?
- What is he or she looking for in employees that get promoted?
- What concrete accomplishments demonstrate that you have these competencies?
- Which areas should you look to improve?

The best way to counter a review you don't agree with? Stay calm and stick to the facts. Ask your manager for specifics, being careful not to sound overly defensive or accusatory. If your boss's facts are incorrect, it's your right to refute them, ideally with documentation of your own. And remember: if you walk into your review confident, open, and well prepared—being clear about what was expected of you and with the specific data showing your accomplishments—you shouldn't have a problem.

Plan ahead. Don't be limited to "I had a great year, end of conversation." You should already be thinking ahead to the next year. After you've reviewed your previous accomplishments and challenges, say to your manager, "Let me tell you what I'm thinking about for the year to come. Here are some developmental things

I'm thinking about, and here's the support I need." Research shows that people who have the broadest set of skills are the ones most likely to survive a downsizing. So what skills might add to your repertoire? A computer course? International experience? An assignment in the marketing department? Now's the time to put it out there by asking explicitly for what you need to grow. Be sure, of course, that whatever you're thinking about is in line with the company's larger objectives.

SHOW ME THE MONEY

Even when the economy is flagging, everything is negotiable—including the size of your paycheck. If you plan well, do the research, and communicate clearly, you can get what you want and deserve.

Sharon Hall, a partner in the Atlanta office of Spencer Stuart, an international executive search firm, is a master negotiator. Here she explains her guidelines for negotiating compensation:

Know your market worth. If you don't know the value of your skills in the marketplace, you give your boss total control during salary negotiation. And your worth has nothing to do what you'd like to make or what you think you should make. You need to know, so get the facts. If you think your market worth is 10 percent higher than what you're currently getting, for example, you should be able to explain why. So talk to friends in your network to find out the general range people are paid in your industry, your position, your region. Do online research. Websites such as Salary.com have very detailed compensation information that's easy to navigate. Take calls from headhunters. Even if you aren't interested in the jobs they're offering, listen, especially when they talk salary. You might hear about something that will surprise you.

Pinpoint what you want. Start from your market worth, and don't be shy. Look your boss in the eye and say, "I want 8.5 percent, because this is what I'm worth, and here's why."

Identify your walking point, your magical price. At what point are you prepared to walk away, to leave the negotiations? And do you have a ready alternative? (In a tight economy or a downturn in your particular area, you need to know what options are available before you play this card.) This information will strengthen your backbone just when you need it most.

Know what your negotiating partner wants and why. While you want more money, he or she might be looking for someone to spearhead a new project or initiative. Could you give your manager what he or she wants in exchange for what you want? See if you can achieve a win-win solution.

Never compare yourself to others. You shouldn't be saying, "I want to make $70,000 because so-and-so is making that much." You can never be fully informed about anyone else's situation. Maybe the other person is making more because she has three degrees and you have only one. Or he's putting eighty hours a week, while you're working ten to six from Monday through Friday. Or she's the niece of the CEO. At the same time, don't allow your boss to compare you to anyone else. Keep the conversation about you.

Manage the dialogue and process, particularly if the discussion isn't going as expected. First, stay calm and agree with your opponent. This usually disarms the other person and prepares him or her to listen. Then state the facts—your market worth and the details of your performance—keeping your emotions in check. Walk your boss over to your point of view.

Finally, be creative. In a tough economic climate, it's generally harder to squeeze out more money. So remember that a raise doesn't have to come in dollars. Consider other areas you are willing to negotiate, such as vacation time, flexible work hours, a better title or office, stock options, or tuition reimbursement.

Take Time Afterward to Process

When you come out of a performance review, exhale and take a moment. Whether the review was great or just okay, go get a cup of coffee and digest the conversation. Look over your notes and think about what you need to do differently—or what you need to do more or less of—to move forward. Make a list of things that are working, as well as areas that need improvement. You also don't have to do this right away. You can also wait for the weekend, so you can relax with a cup of tea or a glass of wine.

GIVE AS GOOD AS YOU GET: THOUGHTS FOR MANAGERS

For most managers, performance reviews feel like a necessary evil—something you know you should and must do but wish you didn't have to do. Like going to the dentist.

Even though you might dread them, performance evaluations can be one of the most important tools in a manager's bag of tricks. It's a structured opportunity to have a conversation with an employee about what he or she is achieving for the department. How well you evaluate your employees can make or break the success of your team as a whole.

My friend Dr. Stella Nkomo used to have to evaluate twenty-seven employees at the end of the year at a previous university position. "It was tedious, and I worried about being fair," she recalls. After a few years of that, she says, "I became a pro." Here's her best advice, based on years of practice, for giving fair, accurate, constructive reviews.

Plan, plan, plan. Most managers don't prepare adequately for the review. You don't start planning the week before. Sit down with each employee a year ahead of time and together come up with a performance plan. This is essential for new hires. Make sure it lists everything she or he needs to accomplish, explains how the employee will get measured, and spells out how the two of you will communicate. So often the trauma in the review comes when you and the employee aren't in agreement as to what the goal was and how it's measured. Planning ahead sidesteps that concern.

Provide lots of feedback. During the year, offer positive, constructive, specific feedback, even if it's informal. When I had all those employees, I sat down two or three times a year with each and asked, "How's it going? Are there obstacles we need to discuss? How can I support you?" It was time-consuming but paid off in the long run.

Keep files. I'm amazed at how many managers have no record of what an employee has done. Hang on to documents related to each of your team members' performance. If it's a negative, be very specific. And don't shock them with a battery of things that have gone wrong at the review. Give them a heads-up when it happens: "You missed this important meeting on this date. I'm making a note. It will impact your review."

Look at your group as a whole. As you prepare for the reviews, pull out the files of everyone on your team and get a sense of how the whole group did. If you do each person individually only, you may overinflate or underinflate.

Allow plenty of time. Don't rush; block out a few days for your process or work on the reviews at home. After you write them up, set them aside for a day or two, and then ask yourself upon reviewing them: "Have I been fair? Do I know everything about each person's performance for the year? Have I evaluated the evidence accurately?" If you have, then you're ready.

Make an agenda for the review. In the end, it's a meeting, like so many others. Think about how you want to structure the conversation. It's generally best to let your employee speak first. Ask, "How do you think your year went? Let's look at your performance plan together." Then listen. After the two of you have spoken, make sure everything's understood and that there's consensus. If there's no consensus, at least make sure what you've said is clear. Do it in a gentle way. As the review winds down, ask, "Do you have any other concerns? What else can I do to support you? Let's think about next year's plan."

Make each review very specific to the employee. On your team there'll be outstanding workers, people who are difficult, and others who need lots of nurturing. Think about what you want to accomplish and work backward. Take your time, listen carefully, and be honest and clear. Use these reviews as opportunities to make your team shine.

It's a Party:
Making the Performance Review Fun

Judy Jackson is senior VP and head of human resources at Digitas, the global marketing and media agency. She is smart, warm, and full of life, and her personality is reflected in the unique and creative ways that she both gives and receives performance evaluations.

––––––––––

At Digitas we have standard review forms, and I do use them. They are for career development as well as to award bonuses. It's very structured and looks at how you performed and the expectations going forward. Basically, it's "Did you meet your goals or not?"

But with my six direct reports, every year I supplement the standard review with something more meaningful. My vision of the review is that it should be a celebration of success, like a surprise party. I take that thought with me when I meet with my people. I imagine that each one is going to walk into the room and get showered with wonderful accolades. People will be singing songs, celebrating you. You get cake. You think, "I can't wait for my performance review."

Because we work for an ad agency, I also try to make something creative for each person and present it as part of the review. Last year I made a poster of quotes for everyone. All of the quotes were positive, highlighting the things that they did well and whatever sound bites distinguished that individual. One year I designed magazine covers with the person's photo and cover lines that talked about the good things. Another year I wrote letters that said, "Let me tell you what's important about you and what you bring to the table."

This year, I'm putting together tape recordings. I'm thinking of something like, "If you're ever feeling down or wonder about how you're doing and what you're doing, here's what's wonderful about you."

This is hard work, but it pays off. It builds commitment and reinforces each person's value. Too often we focus on the negative, the problem areas, with the idea that this will help them grow. But at the end of the day, people who feel special and appreciated are the ones who go the extra mile. And in this economy our currencies are limited. You might not get promoted as quickly, and bonuses and increases aren't the same as they used to be. So you have to find different, more creative ways of rewarding people.

As far as my own evaluation, it's the traditional review. But I will often write my bosses a thank-you letter, telling them how they affect me and thanking them for the growth opportunities and support they've provided me. I remind them that I appreciate the ways they've helped me be stronger and better.

I like surprises, and this always comes as a pleasant surprise to them. Who expects to receive a thank-you letter from an employee, while delivering a review?

I've worked for this company twice, which has given me the opportunity to observe that my boss, the CEO, has changed her review style. Previously she focused on what I needed to work on, so I'd leave feeling a little deflated. It's like, *Will I ever get this right?* Now she concentrates more on leveraging my strengths. The conversation is centered around "Let me tell you what you're doing well, so you can do more of it." She doesn't ignore the weaknesses, but she asks, "How can I put you in situations where you can show your magic?" That feels good.

I work in a tough environment, and it's very busy. Our company is international, and I'm on call 24/7. It's very emotional and sometimes feels like it's never enough. On the days when I wonder, "Why do I do this?" I remember—it's the people.

Performance Review: The Essentials

- *The performance review has changed. No longer a score sheet that looks only at attendance and quality of work, the review can be a valuable tool to help identify and leverage strengths, contributions, and areas of growth.*
- *To be reviewed fairly, you and your manager must be clear—and on the same page—about what's expected of you and how performance is measured.*
- *Set goals for yourself. Make sure that what you are striving to achieve is in line with the company's objectives.*
- *Document everything you do. This is the backup that will help you show that your performance is up to par.*
- *Be open for feedback. During the review, listen without being defensive. If you don't agree, make sure you have the documentation to prove your point.*
- *Know the finer points of salary negotiation. First and foremost, understand what you're worth in money terms by doing research about your position, your industry, and your company.*
- *If you review other people, be fair, prepared, and thorough. Conducting performance reviews can (and should) be time-consuming. But evaluating your employees fairly and thoughtfully can boost the success of your team.*

What's Next?

Remember that feedback is important—not just during the review process but throughout the year. When you try on a dress, you need someone to tell you that it doesn't look good—or that it does. At work, in the long run it's always best to solicit feedback not just from your manager but from other people in the organization whom you trust and who'll tell you the truth. And be self-reflective. Ask yourself, "What is it I need to learn, and how can I improve?"

This feedback, during the review and all year long, will be the secret to moving to the next level. In the chapter that follows, I will explain how to look for, access, and take advantage of opportunities as your career shifts into the next gear.

Chapter 7

Moving on Up: Landing Assignments and Assessing Opportunities

Not long ago at a consulting gig at a large accounting firm, a young woman asked for my advice. This was one of those times when I was forced to give really hard feedback, which isn't an easy thing for me to do. But when you see someone who's placed herself firmly in a box that is cutting off her opportunities and support, the choice is clear.

Right away I took in her poor grooming and defensive stance. Dressed in all black, she looked angry. Her facial expression screamed out, *I don't know if I like myself, but I do know I hate your guts.*

Sitting there with her crossed arms and big scowl, she explained that she was having a terrible experience at a large consumer products company. "I'm good at what I do and work extremely hard, but no one supports me," she said. "I'm not getting key assignments and no one's said anything about how I can advance and get promoted."

"Have you talked to Nancy?" I asked her, referring to a senior manager who's known for supporting and developing younger women. "She could probably give you some advice about what you need to do to get promoted. Why not talk to her or send her an email?"

"Why should I?" replied the angry young woman. "I'm not interested in anything she has to say. She's gotten to where she is by sucking up. Why should she help me? She looks out only for herself."

I told her to sit down. I made it clear that she was being unreasonable and that I wouldn't give her any more advice until she sent Nancy a note and asked her out for coffee. Then I told her to soften her look, to put a little color on. "You're angry and walking around in all black," I said. "You're not going to get noticed or promoted this way. You're scaring everybody to death! Take off the armor, drop your arms, and learn to smile and say good morning."

When I saw her a year and a half later, I didn't recognize her; she was a new woman. Her hair was beautiful and she was wearing a bright burgundy suit. She was smiling and walking with a group of women, and she greeted me with a big hug. She explained that Nancy had given her great advice, and now she also has coffee with other managers in her area. She has volunteered for assignments, she's building relationships, and she has a mentor. Rather than sabotaging herself, she was now doing everything right and positioning herself to advance.

Yes, performance is important, and its value definitely isn't going away, particularly in an age of downsizing and restructuring. If anything, the need to perform has increased dramatically. But as I've discussed in previous chapters—and as I stressed with the young woman above—there's so much more to getting ahead, and even just staying afloat, than hard work alone. As I talked about in Chapter 4, it's critically important to build a unique brand and create buzz about it, particularly in the first ninety days at work. As outlined in Chapter 5, probably this book's meatiest chapter, you've got to grow and maintain relationships at all levels, both inside and outside the company. In Chapter 6, I explained the value of the performance review as an overlooked tool for career planning and development. And finally, as I've stressed throughout this book, especially in Chapter 1, everything you do, in both life and work, is enhanced when you are authentic—honest about who you are and true to yourself.

So if you're really putting these twenty-first-century strategies to work—and I hope you are—your career should be moving forward, whatever that means for you. Still, what other concepts, ideas, and insights might you need to advance your career? I'd like to offer a few other thoughts for figuring out what you want, finding and landing opportunities, and making strategic moves that will propel you to the next level, a different track, or simply keep you strong and secure where you are.

WHERE DO YOU WANT TO GO FROM HERE?

This is the first thing you need to think about in terms of opportunities, assignments, and advancement. So many times we focus only on moving up. It's an American way of thinking that starts when you're young. Advancing through the school system from grade to grade is called "promotion." So it makes sense that later, in our work lives, we still think of advancing as a drive upward toward getting promoted.

But in the harried rush to get ahead—or even just survive—many of us forget to ask ourselves an essential question: "Am I having fun?" The only way to manage continuous cycles in personal development and career growth is to develop your ability to maintain an honest internal dialogue. This is especially true for women. For many of us, up, up, up isn't the answer. Success isn't defined only as a trajectory of advancement that looks like a series of fancy titles accompanied by bigger and bigger pay-checks.

In the short run, think about how you feel right now. If any of the following are true of you, it might be time to think about taking on a new challenge, regardless of whether it will push you upstairs.

- **You're bored.** If you're not challenged or excited and have trouble dragging yourself out of bed, a new assignment might be a refreshing, energizing change of pace. Remember, motivated employees attract more positive attention than those who've grown tired and stale. Don't wait until you're exhausted and burned out to dust yourself off and try something new.

- **You're curious.** Are you interested in something that's going on in your company? A new product or initiative? It might be stimulating to get involved, either on a team, via a new as-signment, or by volunteering for a committee or task force.

- **You're hungry.** No matter where you are in the company, it's important to find opportunities to grow and develop—and not just for those of you who want to be at the top. You should always strive to stay current, with lots of marketable skills and competencies in your tool kit, so explore challeng-ing assignments that allow you to stretch. And in the worst case, in a restructuring environment, you can take those skills with you wherever you land.

In the long run, before you take steps to advance your career, set aside a moment to think about where you want it to go. How do you define success? Please remember that over the years, your definition of personal success may change. You may start out thinking that being the top dog is what you want. Later, you may get involved in a serious relationship and your priorities may shift toward family. (I will discuss work-life balance in depth in Chapter 10.) Or you may realize that doing community work or starting your own business is your true passion. And since the days of the "organization man" who stayed at one job for decades are long gone, you may realize that you want to switch jobs or even fields. What's key, however, is that you define success on your own terms—name it, claim it, create it, and enjoy it.

YOUR EYE IS ON THE PRIZE: THE EXECUTIVE SUITE

If you want to propel your way to the executive suite, be on the lookout for strategic opportunities and be open to assignments that give you added visibility. Succeeding in challenging positions and accomplishing difficult tasks gets you noticed and positioned for the executive suite. But be ready: the high-profile projects that attract attention generally carry added risk. They require you to work on the edge of your skill set, and often mean that you'll need to ask for and work with more resources—money, people, technology. Go after assignments that involve problem solving and are tied to your company's bigger goals, something that answers the questions "What's stopping our company from being all that it can be? How can we make more money? Be on the cutting edge? Move ahead in the marketplace?" Coming up with solutions gets you the goodies. Look for visible, innovative opportunities that play up your creative abilities and allow you to shine.

Ann Fudge is a wonderful case study. I often use Ann as an example of an executive with a knack for turning risky assignments into success stories. In the early 1990s, Ann was the brand manager of the Dinners and Enhancers division of Kraft General

Foods. She was in charge of brands such as Log Cabin Syrup and Minute Rice, favorites of your mama or even grandmother. While these products had high consumer recognition, newer brands were whittling away their market share. In the years that followed, Ann took on the risky challenge of repositioning these and other "old-school" products to a younger generation. Most visibly, she revived Shake 'n Bake and Stove Top stuffing mix for the working-mother crowd, and both products saw large and surprising boosts in sales. Her success in brand turnarounds got her promoted to the position of executive vice president.

In 1994, she took on another tough, risky assignment: rein-venting Kraft's ailing Maxwell House coffee brand at a time when supermarket coffees were being eaten alive by the rise of sophis-ticated outlets such as Starbucks. With a new ad campaign that emphasized durability and retro chic, once again she revived an older brand to highly visible success. (As a footnote that illustrates success on your own terms, Ann has since retired, come out of re-tirement to run an advertising agency, then again stepped out of the limelight and day-to-day corporate life to gain more work-life balance.)

Like Ann Fudge, you must make sure the opportunities that you are looking at to raise your profile are aligned with the com-pany's game plan. In Kraft's case, that meant reviving the sales of older, established, but ailing products. So Ann set her sights on that goal rather than, say, creating a new product from scratch.

This is particularly true in rough economic times. Many com-panies now prize efficiency, reorganization, and cost containment above initiatives such as R & D and other kinds of innovation that cost money. So simply maintaining the position of the company and keeping it viable under tremendous economic strain may be what's valued most. The most visible and valuable thing you might do for your company could be making hard decisions, keeping

your team motivated and productive, managing on fewer resources, and using other perseverance and survival skills to keep
your company strong through the storm. It's important to do the
research to find out where the company's priorities are and get in
line with them.

It helps to find a role model—whether the person knows he or
she is serving that function or not. Look at people in the positions
you see yourself in three years down the road. What was their
journey? Find out what kind of opportunities they had, what issues
they championed, what moves they made. It's great to ask them
directly, but it's also okay if you don't; reading a profile about the
person can be very useful. As you plot your course, keep in mind,
though, that your path probably won't be exactly the same.

Whatever opportunities and assignments you are considering—
or are in the process of grabbing hold of—get prepared. Projects
that are high in visibility, risk, and benefit also carry added responsibility and a greater workload. So get used to working harder
and longer. You might have to pick up and travel with little warn-
ing or be on a conference call to China at 3:00 a.m. You'll also be
under greater scrutiny and pressure. Keeping your relationships
strong is extremely important. You'll need to show that you have
a solid vision and a new strategy that you can communicate to the
people on your team—and that you can get them to deliver. You'll
need to rely on the people in your network, especially when you
get stressed out and need some advice or someone to talk to or
hang with. And you'll have more contact with the people in the
executive suite, where, at best, you'll be headed soon if you're not
already there. So be sure you're ready to show your stuff—you
asked for it!

WHEN THE BEST MOVE IS SIDEWAYS

Promotion doesn't always mean moving up. Sometimes the best career move is lateral. A bigger paycheck and better title are always good. But you can pursue other rewards as well. Exposure, experience, and the excitement of a new challenge can be as gratifying as money and give you a broader skill set in a recession market.

When the economy is down, you may not get as many opportunities to move ahead. So now might be the best time to keep your brand strong and your buzz steady by looking for projects that help you stretch, grow, and gain new skills. You might try to find a lateral move to another area, which could help you see the company from a new angle or perspective. This is the twenty-first-century way of building your career, as the old idea of career silos has died off. In this age of groups and teams and virtual workplaces, the walls are being quickly broken down and people are developing skills and getting experiences in a variety of different areas across functional groups. And you should, too. Remember that your skills and experiences are transferable to other companies, which is valuable given the realities of downsizing and restructuring. You might also look for opportunities that give you global exposure, which I'll talk about in detail in the next chapter.

Remember, too, that down the road, a few horizontal opportunities, projects, and assignments could lead to an upward promotion. So be patient and strategic.

Part of the Career Development Playbook:
A Professional Coach

At some point in your career, you may need an executive or professional coach. Many women hire coaches to help them strategize career advancement and move ahead on the sometimes thorny path to professional success.

Carolyn Henderson is a wonderful executive coach out of Charlotte, North Carolina. Her wisdom is based on thirty years in human resources, specializing in several different areas, including training, development, and compensation. She assumes that all of her clients are high-functioning. Her goal, she says, is to "help them look at their careers through strategic, cultural, and political lenses, and to encourage them to create change and maximize their potential."

Below, I spoke to Rachel Thomas, who is one of seven women from different companies whom Carolyn coaches. Rachel, like the others, is a young, successful woman who would like to be a better leader. In her mid-thirties and a group manager in purchasing for Frito-Lay, Inc. in Plano, Texas, Rachel came to the group very eager and anxious to make some key moves in order to move ahead in her company.

—————————

When I joined the ASCENT coaching group, I had recently been promoted to a managerial position. I was excited about the growth this opportunity would bring and was trying to think ahead to the next career move. Both the one-on-one sessions and the group interactions were very helpful to me as a first-year manager. I needed help with navigating the environment as a new manager, being visible to the organization, and finding ways to talk about career development and expectations. Carolyn provided guard rails when I needed them to successfully navigate the challenges that a new midlevel manager may encounter.

Most useful, I think, was when I reached out to Carolyn around the time of my performance review. I have to admit, I was mainly looking at the review as a way to talk about the next career step. Although I was not immediately ready to make another move, I wanted to make sure the organization was aware of my ambition to grow in different areas of the purchasing function. Right away, Carolyn advised me that while it's great to look ahead, I should enjoy the moment I was in and walk into that light; the next opportunity will come at the right time. "Your manager might not be excited if you're talking so much about the future. Maybe you should bring some of this stuff up later down the road."

I hadn't even thought of how that career ambition could be perceived and was glad that she counseled me on a better way to manage it. I was afraid that if I was not thinking and talking about the next role, the organization would keep me in my current position. It took Carolyn to say, "You aren't even close to that. Calm down and think of a plan. These are the steps you need to take." She also helped me balance the line between sitting around waiting for someone to recognize performance and tooting my horn so much that it seems overbearing or arrogant. I remember her words: "You have to communicate your skills and accomplishments in a way that puts you at the top of mind, so that when opportunities come you'll be thought about." She suggested, for instance, things such as mentioning that I'd taken a class or volunteered for a task force or committee.

Before this experience, I had never thought it would be useful to tone down my ambitions. But now I better understand the value of being a little slower and more strategic as

I think about my career. Carolyn has also helped me think bigger, about my whole life, not just the career. She gave each of us in her coaching group a journal with a handwritten inscription. She has helped me, and all of us, to be more attuned to who we really are and focus on taking good care of ourselves.

BE PART OF A WINNING TEAM

In this climate, teamwork is a major factor in advancement and success. Leading a team may be the best way to shine. Can you pull together a successful team to solve a problem, boost sales, or create a new innovation? Can you delegate responsibilities to make up for areas in which you might not be as strong? If so, explore your group and the company at large for the players you need, communicate your vision, and lead the charge.

On the other hand, a new opportunity may come as an offer to join a team. Can you make winning contributions to a team effort? If so, being a team player might be a great strategic move.

Regardless of your level, but especially if you're more junior and looking upward, here's what a good contributor looks like:

Collaborative. Make sure you understand and show that it's not all about you.

Positive. Don't whine about the work you've been given.

Reliable. Show up on time, informed, and ready to work.

Insightful. Make thoughtful contributions and come up with good problem-solving ideas.

Collegial. This isn't the time to grind an ax or pick a fight. Even if you don't like one or more of your team members, keep it to yourself and focus on the tasks and goals.

Thoughtful. Speak wisely. If you aren't sure, don't talk just to hear your own voice. Contribute when you have something meaningful to add; otherwise wait for the right opportunities.

GETTING INTO POSITION

Just because you're performing, your brand is strong, your buzz is good, and you've built relationships doesn't mean you're going to be bombarded with possibilities. In most cases, you'll have to figure out where the opportunities are and who's doling them out, get yourself into position to receive them, and then ask. Here are some strategies to jump-start the process.

Be vigilant. You have to know not just what's out there but also what's coming down the pike. So often we women are not in the informal networks where decisions get made and assignments are discussed and dealt with. If you have your head down, you're hunched over your desk, and you're not talking to anybody or interacting, plenty of possibilities will fly right over your head. Now's the time to work both your formal and informal networks and contacts in order to get the inside track. What are people talking about? Find out what's going on, who's involved, and what the time line is.

If you're on the lookout for a new position, you'll need to go beyond the job postings. By the time that posting goes up, the upper-ups may already have someone else in mind. If you've done everything right, it should be you.

Spread the word. Keep it positive as you make sure the people in your network—including your manager—know you're interested in a new challenge. One way to show you're ready: volunteer for a task force or a committee, or do a little extra work. That signals that you're motivated, involved, and willing to take on more work, and it raises your profile.

Make sure you're really ready. As you look at different options, take an honest look at yourself. Do you have the skills and competencies to move either up the ladder or laterally? If you're looking at a position in finance because you think that might be good for your career but haven't taken an accounting class since your junior year in college, you most likely need to do some extra work to be a viable candidate. Take a class, read books and financial journals, or do whatever else it takes to make yourself current and prepared. You may have to pay for your continuing education, but in most cases the cost of your career development will be worth the money.

Make your move. Don't be afraid to ask for what you want. So many people, particularly women, want something but are too afraid to ask for it. Pour some passion into your pitch. Tell your manager that you're really interested in this new product or moving into another market—and explain why. Say, "Here are some things that need to be tweaked, and here are some ideas I have."

Be prepared for either a yes or a no. Don't personalize it and get angry if the decision doesn't go your way. Other people are also looking at the same opportunities you're interested in. So you may have to be patient and keep putting yourself out there until you get what you want. Definitely spend no time thinking that you're not good enough or "they don't like me." Keep casting your net. And if you're blessed with a yes, walk through the door with your head held high and with confidence that you're going to be a success.

HOW DO YOU KNOW THE ASSIGNMENT IS RIGHT?

Let's say you get an opportunity or assignment that interests you, or your boss has offered you a new project or position. Before you say (or scream) yes, here a few things to do before you make your decision.

Get clear. Make sure you truly understand what the assignment is and that you and your manager are on the same page. Ask: "What are the expected outcomes? What's the time frame? What support and other resources—people, technology, money— do I have to make it happen?"

Do your homework. Beyond what your manager tells you about the assignment, put your ear to the ground and dig a little deeper. Find out why the company is interested in the initiative or project. How did it come up? If you're in a problem-solving role, make sure the solution to the problem you've been charged with will really lead to a payoff for your area or the company at large. So many times I've seen people work on solving a problem, only to uncover a big, fat iceberg under that small, floating chunk of ice.

Corral support and resources. You must have your manager's support, plus the backing of your manager's manager. And their doors should be open in case you need advice, support, or resources. Make sure you're provided with all the resources to get your mission accomplished, including technology, human capital, and, of course, money. If not, ask for what you need. You need to lock this down *before* you take the assignment, not after.

Push back. Even if you uncover something unexpected or fishy, it might be hard to say no to the opportunity. Instead, think of it as a challenge and push back for more resources or a longer time frame. It's always better to negotiate on the front end than later, after problems arise. And if you do ask for an extended deadline, don't wiggle around the completion; finish on time!

Ask "What's in it for me?" This isn't selfish; it's strategic. Make sure there's a benefit in exchange for hard work, longer hours, more resources to manage, and added risk. On the flip side, ask "What's this going to do for the organization?" That's critical, too.

Be realistic. Can you turn this opportunity into a success? Taking on a challenge is great, but overextending yourself isn't. Make sure you have the competencies and skill sets to take on the assignment. If you're close, think of ways to stretch yourself to gain additional expertise and experience. Just be clear that it's not just your ego saying, "Take it, take it." If you don't have the skill set and can't create a winning scenario, wait for a more appropriate opportunity.

Expect to be afraid. You never *really* know when the assignment is right. It's not as black and white as that. If the thought of the assignment makes you a little uncomfortable, don't back off right away. It's okay to be afraid because you're moving out of your comfort zone. That will help you stretch and grow. So if the voice inside your head is saying, "You can't do that," but it sounds like your scared, little-girl voice, don't give up. Instead, manage your discomfort about doing something new.

Ultimately, remember that it's your decision. If, after you've searched your heart, you can't drum up any energy, excitement, or passion about the assignment, have an honest conversation with your boss. If the opportunity doesn't fit the direction you want to go in the company, doesn't match your brand, or is truly something you can't accomplish, it's not an opportunity at all. Instead, wait for, or seek out, a different challenge or project.

Understand that sometimes you can't say no. During tough economic times, refusing an assignment might cost you your job. So keep your heart and mind open. What happens might surprise you. Look to your network and support team for guidance. You might be thinking, "That's not for me," while someone else—with a fresh eye and ear—might offer a different perspective.

An Opportunity She *Couldn't* Refuse

My coauthor has a friend who found herself confronted with an offer she really couldn't refuse. A high-level executive at a large company, several years ago she watched as a new top management team took over with different ideas and strategies. One by one, many of her peers and colleagues at her level were either forced out or left. She was passed over for a promotion and felt like the last woman standing. Thinking practically, she began considering her exit strategy. But after several months of floundering—and poring over her frayed copy of What Color Is My Parachute?*—to her shock, the new boss called her in and asked her to move to Washington to work in her organization's D.C. office. To her, however, it felt less like a request and more like a command.*

————————

My home and friends—my life—were in New York, and I really had no interest in moving to D.C. On top of that, I had reconnected with an old love, who was moving back to New York the following week from outside the country to try to make our relationship work. How could I tell her, "I know you've moved halfway across the world to be with me, but good-bye, I'm moving"?

But after really thinking it through—and discussing the situation with friends and other people I trusted—I realized I had no choice. Our company was struggling, the victim of the downturn. There would definitely be more restructuring and layoffs. Many of the people I knew had already quit or been pushed out. I was more associated with the old regime; I wasn't in great standing with the new guys, so I had no one looking out for me. My review was below what I'd gotten the year before. I felt lost and my role wasn't well defined. If I refused the offer, I could see the handwriting on the wall.

After much angst, I slapped on a smile and told my boss I'd go. But I wasn't happy. My partner hadn't taken the news well, which threw my personal life into chaos. I had to quickly find an apartment in a new city and move. Worse, I was afraid. Could I succeed in this new assignment? I knew the ins and outs of the company and understood the culture and how things worked—which was why I'd gotten offered the position. But I didn't know jack about Washington. How was I supposed to lead a new team?

My first six months in Washington were beyond hell. I was basically shuttling between the two cities but not living in either. My relationship couldn't survive everything that was going on, and my partner—now my ex—decided to return overseas. I was lonely, unhappy, stressed out, freaked out, and anxious. I felt like an imposter, like any moment somebody would find out that I really didn't know what I was doing. I stopped sleeping and eating to the point where my friends and family started calling and emailing me—and each other—trying to figure out what they could do to help. Several times a day I would think, *What have I done?*

But then something changed. With the '08 election, much of the focus in economics and business shifted to Washington. Where I worked, nobody was prepared for the excitement of the campaign and, eventually, the election of a dynamic new president. Because I had put in the work, I had an edge. I had also gotten myself current and redirected my focus. By the time the recession was in full swing and the mortgage and banking crisis, the bailout, and the Treasury department started to dominate the news, I was in a pretty good position. I'm now surprised to find myself tapped as a Washington "expert," representing my organization on television and radio talk shows.

Though things are much better and I'm on more solid ground, I miss everybody closest to me and wonder how I'm going to get back to New York. But for now, I'm grateful that what looked like a nightmare turned out okay. Better than okay.

WHEN YOU SHOULD LEAVE

You think you're doing everything right, but you've hit the wall . . . or the ceiling. You're doing your job and doing it well. You've got your career plan and a mentor. There's good buzz about you, your network is strong, you've attended professional meetings, your skills are up to date, and your reviews are good. But it's still not happening for you in the company. You aren't getting the signals that advancement is in your future, and you feel stuck. Should you leave?

Maybe. There are times that come down to fish or cut bait. Here's when it's time to consider leaving:

Your manager is not supportive. He or she is sabotaging you by creating terrible buzz, being negative, or going after you.

You've repeatedly been turned down for assignments. You've done the work and asked for new opportunities but have been refused time and again. If you keep getting a no, it might be time to face the reality that it's not going to happen for you. A caveat: for women, it often pays to wait it out. One of the things my coauthor and I discovered when researching our book *Our Separate Ways* is that some women, particularly black women, got promoted because they stayed longer. So have patience and persevere as long as it doesn't feel like suffering and torture.

You start getting bad feedback. Your manager tells you that you're not a team player or that you've haven't demonstrated leadership. You have a file to show otherwise, but you feel your manager's building a case against you. He or she can't give you specific examples of what you're doing wrong. If you can't turn it around within a year, start looking both within the company and outside.

You hate your job. This sounds like common sense, but so many of us are working in companies that we despise. The culture is negative, the environment hostile. You feel disrespected or, worse, are experiencing racial hostility and/or sexual harassment. You get a knot in your stomach when you walk up to the building and it's there until you leave at night. There is no way you can bring your whole, authentic self into that landscape. You cannot shine.

Your company has fallen far from grace. If the integrity of the company is so low that its brand and reputation are going to tarnish your brand and reputation, it's time for you to go.

You've done all that you can do. If being a good corporate citizen isn't enough and you know you're not going to make it into the executive suite at this job, then it's time for you to look for the next dragon to slay. Or your mission's accomplished, your motivation is gone, and you don't enjoy going to work anymore. I've seen this happen to women in the executive suite: they like the culture, the products, and the values, but they've hit a brick wall. So they go to another company where they can work at the next level and have vision, visibility, authority, and power. It's often a competitor. In these cases, it's critical to maintain relationships by holding on to allies, friends, and mentors from the former company. Sometimes, once they see how much you've grown and learned, they'll invite you to come back. Or beg you.

Regardless of *why* you decide to go, before you walk out the door, think about the timing. If you've got a job, benefits, and a salary—maybe even a good salary—does it make sense to stick it out? If the economy is stagnant and there's uncertainty in your industry or everywhere, you might need to tread water until things get better. What's going on at home? Can you afford to leave your job right now if you don't have the next one lined up? Think carefully and strategically before you make any sudden moves.

And don't resign until you've had an honest conversation with your managers and your mentors. See what kind of feedback they give you. You might be thinking, "I'm not wanted, they don't see what I have to bring to the table," while, unbeknownst to you, somebody above you has great plans and intentions for you that you're not aware of.

As you voice your dissatisfaction, don't cry wolf. Don't threaten. It's not a game. If your manager really wants you to stay, think seriously about whether you really are going to stay. Don't fool around. Gamesmanship won't work here.

No matter how hostile the environment, keep yourself together and don't burn your bridges. Leave, but say your thank-yous first. If you're asked to do an exit interview, be honest but not too honest. Do your best to avoid blame and anger. It's always safest to stick to the line "It wasn't a good fit."

If there's a moment between the time you've resigned or been laid off and the time you have to actually leave, make the most of it. Make sure your resume is up to date (it always should be) and talk to as many people as you can both inside and outside the company. Back up your files and take them home. Work your network. If your manager offers to help you build a bridge to new job possibilities, accept.

When the job has ended, don't sit back and moan and groan. Now's not the time to pick up the phone and whine to your friends. Be proactive and walk into the world with a clear focus. Be flexible and realistic. It might take longer than expected to get another job. You may have to move to a different region or switch to an industry you never saw yourself working in.

Please understand that I'm not suggesting you should march out the door. I know you've got to eat and you may have a family to feed. But I am telling you to have courage and to take the risk, knowing that you're talented and there's something else out there. Don't stay put just because you think this is the best you can do. There's always something better, but you have to go out and find it.

Finally, not every exciting, energizing opportunity is directly connected to your job. There may be some of you who are happy, comfortable, and satisfied exactly where you are. If so, you can keep yourself sharp, fresh, and motivated with projects outside of work. Volunteering your time or being involved in sports, church, your children's school, the arts, community activism, or politics can open your heart and your mind. These activities can help you stretch and grow, introduce you to new people, build your skill set, and allow you to be a leader. Success is how you define it. Aspiring higher may not be your measure of success. Part of knowing yourself is understanding what makes you feel fulfilled and having the courage to go after those things that make you happy and whole.

Moving Up: The Essentials

➤ *More than ever, performance is the key to job success.
However, there's more to moving up than simply working
hard. You must also create a game plan, be authentic,
cultivate relationships, and build your brand.*

- *Consider how you define success. What does it look like for you? With this in mind, you might want to aim toward a lateral move that provides an opportunity for you to grow and stretch.*
- *If you want to advance to the executive suite, make sure that you're ready. Start by figuring out where the company's priorities lie and get your own goals in line.*
- *Consider professional coaching. A coach can provide honest feedback and help you strategize your next move.*
- *Leading a team may be the best way to stand out. And being a team player is always a smart move.*
- *Choose assignments carefully. And also understand that sometimes you can't say no when offered an opportunity, especially in a tough climate.*
- *If you've done your best but still aren't getting ahead, think about leaving. But make sure you've thought it through. If getting out is your best option—or your only option—leave with grace.*

What's Next?

In this chapter we discussed assignments and opportunities. As corporations have become global, your greatest opportunity and best chance for advancement may be in another part of the world. The most sought-after jobs are international, and in Chapter 8, I will discuss the benefits and challenges of being a "woman of the world."

Going Global:
Preparing for Success in
International Assignments

At the 2009 Academy Awards ceremony, a little film, *Slumdog Millionaire*, stole all the honors. It tells the story of two brothers growing up in Mumbai. They must overcome every obstacle imaginable: they lose their mother, have to fight wretched poverty, and are hungry, neglected, and abused. But ultimately this heart-wrenching Cinderella tale is an uplifting story of survival against all odds.

After the Oscars, news reports the next day indicated that *Slumdog* had been a hard little film to get a studio to buy. It didn't have any big-time, all-American movie stars. Who cared about two little Indian brothers growing up poor? And subtitles and exotic music? Several years ago, producers and other film execs couldn't see the potential box office mojo in the movie.

But in the end, this film that took place on the other side of the world was the one that captured everybody's heart. And *Slumdog* wasn't the only international Oscar winner: aside from Sean Penn, the lone American, all of the major acting awards went to non-Americans—a British actress, a Spanish actress, and the deceased Australian actor Heath Ledger.

Here's a simple observation based on these Oscar night wins:

the world is becoming a much smaller place. America, its stories, and its heroes are not the center of the universe. And talent, skill, and storytelling that capture our hearts come from all parts of the universe and may even be a welcome relief to some.

Welcome to the global landscape.

We live in a global era. Technology helps to move us across international time zones, puts us in instant communication, and allows us to do business anywhere and everywhere in the world. And if you are serious about being in the executive suite or working in an extreme job, you're going to have to get used to playing on this global field.

In the past few years, it has become increasingly clear that at many companies, in order to reach the uppermost ranks, you will have to take a global assignment. That's not a rumor; it's a reality in the vast majority of American companies right now. Like the studio suits who passed on *Slumdog*, many of us are just coming to terms with this reality. Executives often complain that it's extremely hard to get women to take international assignments. Some of the reasons are understandable.

Some of us are afraid to live in a foreign country, fearful of the isolation and loneliness that can come with living abroad. Others are concerned that the company will forget about them and they'll lose career traction being so far away. If you're already feeling invisible in the workplace and no one is aware of you, you may fear that leaving the country may put you completely out of sight and out of mind. Other women worry about getting back home once they leave. How do you negotiate reentry from halfway around the world?

But the biggest issue concerns family, which you'll read about in detail in Chapter 10. Women, even those of us who aren't married and don't have kids, have to maintain an extensive and extended constellation of people we take care of and are responsible for. We are the hubs of family and friend networks and are called upon to be advocates, caretakers, resource providers, and surrogate parents for children, parents, and other relatives and friends. Being pulled across the planet for a long period can cause the whole network to collapse. Living outside of the region is difficult enough, but adding an international time zone may prove too hard to manage.

If you're married or in a committed relationship, what do you do about your partner? Can your mate relocate, especially if he or she has a good job already? What about your kids? How will they adjust? Where will they go to school? If you're single, will you be safe by yourself in an outpost in the Middle East? In a war zone? How will you maintain your spirituality and everything else that keeps you grounded in a foreign country?

Then there's my favorite: where will you get your hair done? That can be a problem when you move across the country, much less around the world. For many women, especially those of us with natural hair, hair that needs to be relaxed, and the like, that really is an issue.

Even if you aren't willing or able to relocate to another country, in the new global landscape you must cultivate skills that cross borders (which includes speaking different languages) and learn to function on a twenty-four-hour clock. Global jobs demand travel and technological literacy. Don't be surprised if you have to get up at 2:00 a.m. for a conference call with a company based in Ghana or Indonesia. You must also be flexible and open enough to appreciate and engage effectively with other cultures.

Below, I will discuss how to leverage the career advantages and disadvantages of a global assignment, and I'll offer advice for becoming a global citizen, including how to build an international network. Through first-person stories we'll look at the realities of both living abroad and taking on a globe-trotting international assignment.

HOW TO MAKE YOURSELF A WOMAN OF THE WORLD

Everyone needs to be a global citizen. What does that mean? More than eating sushi and going to Club Med on vacation. Whether you take an international assignment or your company simply does business overseas—or is planning to—here are some things you can do to make yourself more internationally literate.

Study up. Don't skip over the international pages of your newspaper or newsmagazine or tune out when NPR or CNN runs features about other countries. Know what's going on in the world. Pay particular attention to the countries where your company does business. Who's the president or prime minister? What are some of the governmental issues? What makes the culture unique?

Understand where your company fits in the international marketplace. This is good information to have that will help you strategically. Find out how your company is positioned internationally and how that will change in the next few years. You can ask your manager or mentor or simply listen and learn. It might be as simple as checking your annual report or reading news reports. Find out, too, what kinds of international firms your company works with. And what's the global outlook for your competitors?

Get out and travel. With the money you're probably making, you can afford to travel. Go abroad so that you can learn about other cultures and see them for yourself. Plan summer trips, and try to go with your family—your mate, your children, your god-children, your mother.

Learn a foreign language. After teaching for years in top-ten business schools, I'm amazed at international students' grasp of the English language. And it's not just when they speak: their writing in English is amazing—they're better than many of the American students. It's impressive. Most of my American students couldn't debate, deliver arguments, participate in class, then present a project in a language other than English. Even if you never become fluent, it's good to know another language.

Understand cultural innuendos. This is particularly true if you're going to work on an international team. American culture is very reactive, outspoken, and individualistic. We pride ourselves on speaking out and getting our point across. But there are Eastern cultures that are more reflective. They don't talk just to talk. They don't have to argue their points. At my school, some of my American students complain that their Asian counterparts, for example, don't participate fast enough. But it's because they're thinking.

Learn to be culturally sensitive and competent. Other cultures have different styles of interacting, body language, and ways to express their feelings, and that doesn't make them inferior to yours. If you end up overseas, being an "ugly American" will get in the way of your success.

Be flexible. If you're living here but have an international orientation, get accustomed to working different hours. Don't demand, for example, that the teleconference be scheduled for hours most convenient to you. Work on your overseas colleagues' time frame. It should be give-and-take. I know of a woman who was complaining on and on about a weekly 2:00 a.m. conference call to Asia. "Why can't they be on our time?" I remember her bellowing. Guess what happened to her? She was shown the door.

Seek out people who come from different places. Make sure some of your workplace allies come from other parts of the world. And do your best to include people from abroad in your extended network and social circles.

When an International Job Takes Life by Storm

Meet Jessica C. Isaacs, senior vice president at a global insurance company. This longtime insurance pro, one of the most powerful in the country and perhaps the world, talks about how, as she puts it, she "accidentally landed in an international career."

————————

During undergrad and at law school, I was an intern at Allstate Insurance Company. I had never considered a career in insurance as my goal. My plan, and that of my father, was for me to become a lawyer. However, after I was finished with law school, Allstate offered me a position and I took it. So at twenty-one, I began a career and was one of the company's youngest managers.

Over the years, I worked in claims, I was a district sales manager, and ultimately I became a regional underwriting manager. I didn't realize it at the time, but to have the exposure in all of those areas was excellent training and laid a great foundation for my future. That experience gave me a total understanding of the business. During that time, I moved many times, from Atlanta to Chicago to D.C. and back to Chicago, and I also found the time to get married.

While in D.C. in 1992, I had a big career moment. I was asked to be a member of the White House Task Force for Hurricane Andrew. It was very newsworthy that Allstate had somebody at the table, and my company took note, all the way to the highest levels. That recognition and exposure were just what I needed. I had been working hard along the way but was hardly noticed. Shortly afterward I got promoted to regional manager and moved to New York. That high-profile appointment also led to the call from a headhunter that changed everything for me.

The headhunter was looking for someone with a strong consumer-lines insurance background for an international insurance carrier. I told her I wasn't interested mainly because I was still living out of a suitcase in temporary housing during my actual move to New York. The thought of an international career was exciting, but the timing was just not right. I would read about people with international careers, but in 1992, I didn't know anyone who actually had one.

My international exposure had been during my travels to the Caribbean, and I had been to London and Paris once. I had taken French in high school and college but was not considered fluent. That was the extent of my international experience. The headhunter convinced me to go for an exploratory interview, and I was selected for the job.

By then it was 1994. My company already had operations in Japan and other parts of Asia and was looking to expand into emerging markets in Latin America and Southeast Asia. My job was to develop strategic plans and build the infrastructure to distribute personal-lines business in these markets by exporting my insurance knowledge and best practices internationally. I started by building business all over Latin America and the Caribbean. Then my responsibility grew and I began traveling to Germany, the United Kingdom, and Ireland. Now we're also in South Africa, Kenya, and Uganda. I was traveling probably 55–60 percent of the time: one week here, get clean clothes, another week there. I knew all the flight attendants by name and they knew me.

Though I love my job, there have been sacrifices. Several years ago—after more than eight years on the road and more than one million frequent flyer miles—I made some changes. One day when I was at home, somebody asked me, "Do you know this person in New York?" I said no. "That person in New Jersey, where I live?" And I said no. I started feeling like something was missing. With all the travel, I didn't have time to develop friendships outside of work, to network, or to join organizations. I was this African American female insurance executive running something big, and no one knew who I was—and I didn't know anybody.

I decided to create a better work-life balance for myself. I joined the Executive Leadership Council, a professional networking organization with more than four hundred senior-level executives as members. I joined the boards of several nonprofits and started giving back to my community. And yes, I began meeting a lot of new people and developed many new friendships.

While I still love my international career, I've cut back on my travel and found time to fit other things, including friends and family, into my life. This has allowed me to have more of a balance between my career, my home, and my community involvement.

Sometimes I feel as though I got into an international career by accident. Someone once told me about all of the things that should be obstacles for me—that I'm African American, female, not fluent in all languages, and am often explaining something nobody knows anything about. But I wasn't buying it. I think it's really about performance, which is the great equalizer. I know the business and do my job well and deliver, which takes things like sexism out of the equation. I also try to be professional and optimistic and to value people's opinions.

In this day and age, if you're thinking about an international job or a global assignment, I say go for it! Many U.S. companies are expected to grow, and most will need to look internationally. Many of them have their sights on the emerging markets or the BRIC countries—Brazil, Russia, India, and China. Having international credentials can be a game changer in the future.

THE JOYS AND CHALLENGES OF AN INTERNATIONAL OPPORTUNITY

Do you need to have a global assignment? The answer is probably no. I know plenty of high-level women who work for international companies but have never lived abroad. But it doesn't hurt if you can. And it benefits you if you do. Living and working overseas expand you in ways you cannot imagine, exposing you to opportunities and places you never, ever thought you'd see. It also changes your own self-perception and allows you to grow, stretch, and learn.

Still, don't pack your bags before you've thought it through.

Make sure you know what you're getting into. One of my mentees works at a company that's been doing more and more global business over the past decade. So she put out the word that she was interested in an international position. Eventually she was asked to consider working in an East European country. But before she even thought about it seriously, she did her research and called the State Department. In short order, she found out that safety was an issue for a single woman in that particular country. There was actually a travel alert. So she said no and decided to wait for the next opportunity to arise.

Consider how the assignment fits into your career and life plan. If you're not sure you want to move, think about whether you really need it to advance. Does it fit into where you see yourself headed in the next five years, or would another kind of project benefit you just as much? Look at other top executives—did they work overseas? What about your family? If you have a very elderly mother or father, now might not be the best time. If you have little kids, now might be better than when they're older and in school. Can your husband or partner get a sabbatical? Think creatively but realistically.

Get to know the country. Don't get swept away by the idea of a place. Understand the reality. Learn about the geography, history, and political and economic issues. The easiest thing to do right away? Look at a map. Second, talk to someone who's lived there— if possible, someone else from your company or in your field.

Do the hard work to make sure your immediate family and extended network are on board. Obviously, if you're partnered and have children, these are the first people you'll talk with before you decide for sure. If it's manageable, involve the rest of your family in the process. Consider a family meeting with everyone involved—those who are going plus those who aren't. Discuss the changes, the time frame, the shifting responsibilities, the challenges. It helps to get everything out in the open and share as much information as you can. For those who are being uprooted—like your kids—get them prepared as early as possible.

A woman I know was transferred to her company's office in Moscow. Her children knew six months ahead of time and were talking about it, learning to speak Russian, and sharing information with their friends. On the last day of school, her son's class gave him a good-bye party and gifted him with a memory book of photos with everyone's photos, addresses, and emails, which made leaving a little easier for him.

See if you can tweak the assignment. Do you have to live there, or can you travel back and forth like Jessica Isaacs, the insurance executive mentioned earlier in this chapter? It might be better to break it up. Maybe you could be in Brazil for three months, get your work done, and then spend several months at home. Or go for a year or less.

Negotiate the terms of your return before you take off. It's always best to nail down a strategy for your return before you get on the plane. My coauthor has a friend who was a high-level manager for a large clothing corporation and was sent to her company's office in Milan. Lucky her: she loved food and wine and travel, so this was an ideal assignment. Despite some initial bumpiness in the first year as she strived to improve her high school Italian, eventually she came to love her job. She made lots of friends, both Italians and other expats, and had an active social life, including lots of travel around Europe.

After a while, however, she felt like she was losing touch with friends and family back home, and missed the United States fiercely. She was ready to return. But in the seven years she had been away, her company had tightened up and her previous manager had been downsized. Back home, there was no slot—either at her level or above—open to her. She felt stuck, knowing that she would have to either wait it out or quit and start fresh.

After a year, a position finally opened up, but in a different area and a bit lower on the food chain. To get back to the States, she took it, but not happily. Now, several years later, she has gotten on track. Though she sees her years in Italy as some of the best of her life, she wishes she'd thought to put a reentry strategy in place.

Use your company as a resource. Relocating is always overwhelming, so be sure to tap into whatever your company can provide—travel and moving logistics, other people to talk to, community resources, school and living information, language classes, and so on.

Learn the norms of the culture. That includes etiquette, social customs and behavior, and business practices. Really observe. Understand native foods, appropriate gift giving, how to make introductions, leadership style, and anything else you can pick up. Also remember that the way men deal with women—and women deal with other women—may be different in your host country. Keep in mind that if you're a woman of color, people in your new country may not have had a lot of experience with those who look like you. Do your best to build on your uniqueness in a natural, holistic way.

Don't isolate yourself, especially if you're single. You're there to work, but it gets lonely, and you should have a social life, too. Build social networks in your new home, both inside and outside your company. Be sure to mix and mingle with as many people as you can, other Americans included.

Keep up with the latest technology. Skype, anyone? You're going to need to keep in contact with your friends and family and stay abreast of what's going on at home. It's probably a good idea to help your loved ones here get current with their international technology. At minimum, make sure everybody has email and international phone cards.

Plan for your reentry. Don't wait until you're on your way home. Six months before your return, begin talking to your managers and your mentors about the best position for you stateside. That might mean making a couple of visits back home to discuss the new skills and insights you've acquired and how you can best use them when you return.

A Free-Spirited Banker Living
and Working in London

Over a year ago, one of my students moved to London for love and then found a career there. A business manager for an international bank, she is impetuous, a spontaneous kind of person who thinks having a five-year plan is a waste of time. Here's how she ended up across the pond.

———————

I am from Mexico and went to college and law school there. After I figured out that I didn't want to be a lawyer, I went to work with my dad at his event management company. Event planning is kind of fun, but working the auto show isn't exactly what I wanted to do. So I came to the United States and got my MBA.

Once I graduated, I wasn't sure what I was going to do. I liked finance, but I wasn't convinced about the investment banking idea. And corporate finance and accounting both sounded awful. People always told me I should work with people, something that involves the client. I thought of wealth management. It was very broad, sounded glamorous, and was all about the client.

Even as I was still trying to figure out what I wanted to do as far as my career, I started dating a guy I really liked. He was moving to London, so I started looking for opportunities in Europe. People thought I was off the wall, but I decided to give it a shot with him, and moving felt right to me.

I got an offer in Spain, but then I'd be commuting. So I ventured to London without a job. It was crazy: my job search barely lasted a week. Through a friend, I heard that they needed people at a large bank ASAP. I met the guy who is now my boss, and after ten minutes I ended up with an offer. I started work before my boyfriend.

I don't mean to make it sound totally easy. The first few weeks I had all kinds of second thoughts. I'd come to be with this guy and decided to charge forward—was that a mistake? He was the only person I knew, and he was working twenty-four hours a day. I had no friends, no family, and no support system. It wasn't any better at work; the first week I thought, *Am I underqualified for this position?*

I went to my boss and said, "I have no idea what I'm doing. This job is kicking my ass." He was blunt but kind. "If you want to be nurtured and have a comfortable start," he said, "then this is the wrong job. We want you here and we want you to succeed. But you need to pick up this job as quickly as you can. And know I'm here to help."

That made sense. I was able to see that now was the time to push myself, to get experience and make mistakes. I'm thirty-two and don't have responsibilities and kids to worry about, so this is the right time for me to be working hard and living abroad. That little change in my mind-set made all the difference.

I've been in London for a year and a half, and my career has taken off. My manager nominated me for this program where they give you a high-profile mentor, offer leadership seminars, and pay for training and certification. I feel like being here has opened a lot of doors. And really, the culture shock for me was probably easier than it is for other Americans. I had already been through that when I moved to the States from Mexico. My internship for business school was at a company in a small midwestern city. I felt more like a fish out of water living in small-town America as a Mexican than I do here.

Plus London has so many expats. I work in the international part of the bank. In my immediate group, there's only one person's who's British. There are people from all over the world. The hardest part is being so far from my family in Mexico. The plane ride home is eleven hours. I lived at home until I was twenty-six, so I talk to my mom five days a week.

I don't know how long I'll be here. I don't have a five-year plan; I think they're stupid. Sometimes you need a little bit of a shake-up . . . and a lucky string of events.

Going Global: The Essentials

- *If you're serious about being in the executive suite, it's increasingly important to make sure you're part of the international landscape. At minimum, you must cultivate skills that cross borders, such as speaking another language.*
- *Know where your company fits globally. And seek out coworkers from other countries.*
- *If you're interested in an international assignment, understand what you're getting into. Start by doing research. And consider carefully how living outside of the United States will impact your personal life and your family.*
- *While overseas, work hard (of course) but don't isolate yourself. Build networks and take advantage of your unique experience.*
- *Before you're ready to come back home, negotiate your terms for reentry into the country and the company.*

What's Next?

Across the globe—whether in New York City, Hollywood, Mumbai, Beijing, São Paulo, or Johannesburg—it is no longer just the CEO who directs the company. The most successful corporations have strong leaders at every level. A good leader communicates a clear vision, develops others, can function in several if not all areas of the company, manages well up and down, shares power and recognition, and must be willing to take strong stances. She or he is also open and open-minded, has a good deal of self-awareness and self-knowledge, and is comfortable in her own skin. The next chapter will discuss all that it takes to be a good leader and the importance of developing others in order to develop yourself.

Chapter 9

Effective Leadership in the New Corporate World

Afew years ago, I consulted for a large company and got to know a woman who was a top manager, in charge of a major department. Brilliant and charismatic, she had been recruited from a big corporation outside of her industry, and she came in with a lot of buzz.

Right away I wondered if she was going to make it. In her mid-fifties, she was very traditional and her leadership style seemed outdated. People were in awe of her and she got them excited, but she wasn't good at sharing information. She also worked hard at building her own domain but hadn't adopted the newer, more teamwork-driven leadership model and was less skilled at developing others. Her people felt left out of the information loop and questioned whether they were valued.

This woman, as successful as she had been and might have still been, had been socialized in the old system. In the previous model, you didn't share information, and affirming your employees when they did something right, while important, wasn't key. Success was individual, and when you achieved it, you kept that close to your heart. You built your own empire and didn't seek help.

These types are still out there; you can find them in middle management right now. Many are preparing for retirement. They have trouble being advocates, supporters, and team players. They have only one formula and don't think there are other ways of leading. Younger people don't see themselves in these older peers. They don't seek them out, and instead find ways to go around them.

Down the line, this woman realized that things had changed too much. She put in her letter of resignation and disappeared. I often wonder what became of her.

Leadership has changed over the past twenty years. It's no longer common or desirable for a leader to be an old-school father or mother figure who makes decisions in a vacuum like the autocratic dictator of a small country. In fact, as the structure of corporations has changed and companies have become more complex, global, driven by technology, and run by teams, it's clear that leadership can no longer be a top-down enterprise. Everybody at every level is a leader, not just those in the executive suite. Ordinary people do astounding things in companies and in the world. You don't have to be a leader all the time, but there will be opportunities in your life when you will step into a leadership role. When those opportunities arise, don't be afraid. Lift your head, straighten your shoulders, and walk right in.

Here's what leadership isn't. It's not dictatorial, authoritarian, or "all about me." It's not about big ego: "my way or the highway"–style thinking. It's not about greed, buckets of money, or a big paycheck. Fame, title, and status don't necessarily come with being a leader. Don't confuse being a leader with being a corporate star. It's not always about fighting and competition. It isn't masculine—it's not purely rational, linear, or hierarchical.

Leadership is expansive, innovative, and creative. Good leaders give people hope and have faith. This approach is known as "servant leadership." Servant leaders have integrity and take responsibility. They can communicate their vision and show their feelings, including compassion, concern, and even love.

In this chapter, I offer a set of principles that inform good leaders, and especially the great ones. In shaping this list, I asked the second-year students in my Leadership Out of the Box course for help. They are young, bright, engaged, and thoughtful—and understand clearly that the model of leadership is different than it was in my day. They are the women and men who are poised to become tomorrow's leaders. Together, these are the guiding principles we came up with. They are at once old-school and time-tested but tweaked for our century with its rapid changes and complicated challenges.

As leaders, each of us is a work in progress. I hope you will apply these ideas at work, in your community, and even at home—and add your own special spice to make your leadership style your own.

Bringing All of Her "Selves" to Work

Carla Harris is one of the most powerful and successful women on Wall Street. She executed the IPOs for UPS and Martha Stewart Living Omnimedia as well as the $3.2 billion common stock transaction for Immunex, one of the largest biotech common stock offerings in U.S. history. I admire Carla not just for her high-level accomplishments but also for her down-to-earth leadership style. She has a wealth of self-knowledge and is comfortable in her own skin, which can be a challenge in the white-shoe finance circles in which she operates. When she walks in the door of Morgan Stanley, she brings her whole self—including Carla the gospel singer. Here, she talks about some of *the leadership qualities she found useful recently when she switched to a new area of her company.*

————————

I think I always had leadership qualities. I believe in respecting other people and that everybody has a contribution, no matter what their title is. I'm always willing to admit I've made a mistake and to say I'm sorry. I think people respect that. None of that has changed. That's me. Over the years, however, I have also learned to understand, claim, and own my own power. Although it might sound strange, when you do that it makes you more humble.

Not long ago, I put these ideas into practice. I moved from the investment banking side to investment management at my company. I now have five people reporting to me but am widely seen as a leader on the floor.

This was a new area for me, and I put it right out front. I went in on a mission and approached everyone in the new area with a lot of enthusiasm. I told people, "I'm still learning, but I'm learning as fast as I can. You teach me, I'll teach you." I was the first one in, the last to leave. I may have been well known and successful in the company, but in this area I needed to prove myself before I could really lead.

I think the other thing that worked for me, and always has, is that when I come in, I bring in all of me. That means Carla the investment banker. Carla the motivational speaker. Carla the intellectual. Carla the singer. Carla the philanthropist. These are all facets of who I am, all parts of me that I'm deeply connected to. Being authentic, I think, has helped me form relationships with my managers, with my team, with clients; I never know which Carla somebody is going to connect with.

TWELVE GUIDING PRINCIPLES OF LEADERSHIP

1. Self-Awareness

The strongest leaders are authentic and real and have a keen self-awareness. As I detailed in the first chapter and have stressed throughout this book, you must know who you are and bring your whole self to the table every time. The most admired leaders are empathetic and thoughtful, sometimes through painful experience, reflection, and introspection. This personal evolution makes them understanding and compassionate toward others and allows them to connect. Part of self-knowledge is seeing your shortcomings, which I prefer to call "growth edges." These are the areas in which we need to stretch. So while you need a deep knowledge of the areas in which you lead, allow yourself to always be in learning mode, a perpetual student.

2. Vision

Leaders must have a clear vision—of the organization that they're leading, of the project they are handling, of the goals they are striving for. Effective leaders are problem solvers. They look at a situation and strive to make it better, to make it right. They can take what seems like nothing and turn it into a brilliant idea that will help a company, a community, or a country be a better place.

In this era, solving problems has grown much more complex, as you well know. You must analyze complicated situations and identify multidimensional solutions. These solutions must be based on both data and observations—what you know and what you see. So creating your vision will not be a quick and easy process; it will take deep thought and study, exploring, and listening, combined with reflection and patience.

It can't just be about the moment. Visionary leaders look down the road to see what will happen in the future. Think of Martin Luther King Jr. and his "I Have a Dream" speech. It is remembered as one of the most important speeches in history and positioned Dr. King not only as a champion orator but also as one of the great visionary leaders in all of history. When he tells the world "I have a dream that my four little children will one day live in a nation where they will not be judged by the color of their skin, but by the content of their character," his vision is focused decades ahead.

At this writing, we are mired in the toughest economic era since the Great Depression. As you shape your vision, remember that you may be charged with both solving the problems of right now and also creating goals and dreams for a future that will look much different.

3. Communication

Anyone can have a dream. But a dream that nobody knows about is only a daydream. A leader must communicate the vision, paint it with beautiful broad brushstrokes, then fill in the details for everyone to grasp. A great leader, like Dr. King, can articulate the vision with so much passion, energy, and enthusiasm that people—sometimes millions of them—hitch their wagons to it. It is more than simply having charisma. A lot of leaders can fill a room and give a good speech. But the great ones motivate people and inspire them to *do* something. When you communicate antici-pation, hope, and excitement, you inspire the people around you to take action, make change.

Society is also different now, much more heterogeneous and

fragmented than in the past. These changes demand that you reach out across borders and boundaries, sometimes via technology, to connect, communicate with, and mobilize multiple constituencies, often across cultures, languages, and time zones. Communication should be two-way, and masterful leaders listen to what others have to say, often these days through email. That input allows you to develop and expand your vision.

4. Results

Leadership is more than just talking a good game. You have to deliver results, show that you can get things done, make things happen. That is the key to keeping your company's brand strong, the best in its niche. A good leader uses forward-thinking strategies to develop reliable quality products that meet the needs of the consumer. Think of Apple: even in a recession, iPhone sales are humming. Leaders also recognize that results and success shouldn't come at the price of the community or the environment. Good companies care about the earth, its water and air, and the people who live on the planet, and they give back.

5. Integrity

True leaders believe in the cause and keep their promises. They have to make tough decisions and can't pass the buck to anybody else. You must have the integrity to stay committed to your convictions and values. Leadership isn't a popularity contest. You'll have to make calls some people are not going to like. The important thing is that people feel you have acted for the good of the company and their livelihood.

In our modern era, there is a different level of transparency that runs through our society. In the past, leaders had their shadows, though they might never be revealed. FDR suffered from painful polio that caused partial paralysis in his back, arms, and hands. But, by and large, the public never knew. Today, with bloggers, YouTube, twenty-four-hour cable television, and all the other media, you can't hide.

So do what you say you're going to do. Then open the doors so that it's clear what you're doing and how you're doing it. True leaders don't keep people in the dark; they shine a light so that everybody's part of the process and the solution.

6. Humility

Increased transparency means that all of us have become skilled at looking past the BS, sniffing out what is false. A leader needs a good balance of self-confidence and humility for many of us to respond. The strongest leaders lack arrogance and an overriding ego. They don't take themselves too seriously, and they can ask, "How am I doing?" As a leader, you must treat your followers, your team, with the grace and respect they deserve. You aren't better than them, and they aren't there to serve you. In reality, leaders are the ultimate servants—humble servants.

7. Teamwork

In companies around the world, being able to be a team player and work on a team is more important today than any time in history.

Your team provides more support than you can imagine. They will give you feedback, to help shape your vision and make it better. Leaders have to listen to everyone—the people who are nodding in agreement as well as the naysayers. Learn to listen not just to the usual suspects but to the unusual ones as well. They're the ones who make you think, who can take an idea and turn it upside down and inside out in order to make it better.

You must develop your team; that's how you give back and also how you succeed. The first step in developing your team—as individuals and as a unit—is by developing yourself. If you put yourself through the growth process, then everyone else will be more willing to grow and stretch, too. Leaders must also provide resources for the team, so that you can do the work together. Resources come in many forms—technology, human capital, and money, to name a few. It's up to you to set the tone and shape the culture. You must set the bar high enough to motivate your team members and also recognize and honor their individual and group accomplishments.

Leaders have peers, mentors, guides, coaches, and teachers. They know they can't do it by themselves. Superwoman and Superman don't exist. Leaders don't micromanage; they delegate. They can let go.

8. Influence

We live in a time when you can't offer as many rewards as in years past. Hiring may be frozen, promotions scarce, and bonuses gone. Restructuring, cutbacks, and global competition have left fewer employees working harder and longer than ever. You can't *force* the people you have to work hard and well; you must persuade them. Good leaders must know how to influence people—to create allies and build relationships. You can't hold grudges or be stuck in a power play. Leaders must respect people and pay attention to what they have to say. Even if you don't agree, a leader must at least understand different points of view and be able to listen not only to friends but to foes, too. It's not just internal; you have to be able to influence externally and often globally.

9. Commitment

Leaders are committed. You have to be in for the long haul, until the job's done. You can do other things, take a break, and accomplish the same goals in a different place, but you must have the commitment to see things through.

People won't follow you unless they understand that you aren't just in it for yourself. In your words and your actions, you must prove that there's something for them, too. You especially can't be here today and gone tomorrow. Commitment builds trust, which has been and always will be a cornerstone of effective leadership.

10. Passion

In leadership, you have to have passion. My students often tell me they wish they could find their passion. They're chasing it, like it's something outside of them. Passion is inside of us. I think Derrick Bell, the author and law professor, said it best. He is a wise and gracious man and one of my heroes. (And yes, I love his surname!) His book *Ethical Ambition: Living a Life of Meaning and Worth* (Bloomsbury, USA) is required reading for my students. About passion, he writes: "I understand, of course, that for many the journey to uncover and affirm their heart's passion requires what may appear an endless search. . . . [But] I won't pretend that 'finding your passion' is the key that will unlock the mysteries of all life's issues. That's not passion—that's magic, and as far as I know, it doesn't exist. I can say, though, that passion is an energy that already exists inside each of us."

I think of passion as a tiny seed that was planted in us some-where along our life journey. It was often something that amazed us as a child, so we wanted to be a part of it. It could be seeing a first ballet or baseball game, a trip to a farm or another country. It might be a visit to a hospital or to the vet. Some of you played office with your baby sister as your secretary. You rearranged your room into cubicles and made your little-girl friends into colleagues. You visited your father's or mother's office and the seed was planted. These are the seeds that inspire a deep interest, curiosity, and significance inside of us.

11. Courage

Like all leaders, you will get knocked down, especially now. At the highest levels particularly, everything you do is open to criticism and scrutiny through numerous media and communication channels. People and groups fight for competing wants and needs.

You have to have the strength to get back up, the courage to stand tall, stick to your vision, and do the work that needs to be done to make things better. Leaders have to be able to withstand the loneliness, the challenges, the nitpicking and criticism, and—under the worst of circumstances—the attacks. You need courage to rise above the petty fray, stick to your principles, and fight against what's wrong and for what's right.

I turn again to Derrick Bell for inspiration. I love his thoughts on courage: "Courage is not a quality you have or don't have; nobody is born courageous, nobody has courage all the time, and nobody who has not yet been courageous lacks the possibility of choosing it in the future. Courage is a decision you make to act in a way that works through your own fear for the greater good as opposed to pure self-interest. . . . Courage is our tool in vanquishing fear, but it's not always an easy tool to use, and truth be told, it's rarely glamorous. It's a daily decision to wake up and try to do the right thing, no matter how big the reward or how great the fear."

You must have the courage to dream big and also chase the dream. A strong leader is willing to put herself or himself out there, knowing it's not going to please everyone.

12. Faith

Finally, some of us overlook, both in leadership and in work, more generally the idea of faith. It's not about what church, temple, synagogue, or mosque you attend. It's about having a deep faith in the goodness of humankind and a drive to do better and be better. It's about caring for others, giving back to society, and trusting that any crisis will turn itself around. Though it's rarely talked about, leaders have to have faith. When inspired by faith, leadership brings a deep, deep sense of satisfaction and wholeness.

LEADERSHIP CASE STUDY: *THE LION KING*

Above, I've discussed what it takes to be a great leader. I'd like to illustrate many of the principles with an unusual case study of leadership styles and development: *The Lion King*. One of my dear colleagues, Dr. Lee Bolman, recommended that I look at the movie through the prism of leaders and leadership. Here's my spin on *The Lion King* as a case study in leadership.

On the first day of my leadership class, I show the animated movie to my students. Watch it yourself, and you'll be surprised how vividly the principles of leadership come to life.

I start with Mufasa. With his booming voice and gorgeous, majestic mane, he leads his kingdom with authority, integrity, and vision. Under his leadership, the Pride Lands flourish. Plant life is lush, streams clear, food plentiful—it's a beautiful part of the jungle. The animals are content. Mufasa also has a deep sense of faith; he believes in the Circle of Life.

Looking to the future, he walks his son, Simba, through the Pride Lands, teaching him the principles that the young cub will need to succeed him one day. Mufasa asks his son to look up into the sky, to the great kings of the past, reminding him of his responsibility and his legacy.

When Mufasa is murdered by his brother Scar, who then takes over, things go terribly wrong. Scar—who would name a child that?—is stuck in the ugly. He is wounded and lets his rage, shame, and jealousy consume him. He's got a chip on his shoulder and an ax to grind. He is greedy and has no integrity or commitment. His vision of leadership is about taking over, controlling, war, destruction, and inflicting pain. He creates an alliance with the unethical hyenas, the baddies, and is abusive to the lionesses. Notice what happens to the Pride Lands under Scar's leadership? They become parched and barren. With no food, the animals leave. When there's a leader who's good, life is good—not just for the king but for everybody. When there's a leader who's not noble, who cares only for himself and has no integrity, nothing thrives.

To get rid of Simba and grab Pride Rock, Scar convinces the young cub that he was responsible for his father's death and recommends that he flee. Though young Simba was tutored by his father, he isn't ready to lead. Even as he sings, "I just can't wait to be king," it's clear he's not prepared. He has an immature vision of leadership. He's excited that everybody's going to be afraid of him, though he can't yet roar.

That makes it easy for Scar to set him up. Consumed by guilt and shame, Simba can't face his mother or the other lions. He feels he has no choice but to go away. We learn from Simba that you can't be a leader all the time. You aren't necessarily born to be a leader; it's a journey. Simba runs to a faraway desert, where he can hang out with new friends and be *hakuna matata*, worry-free.

The turning point comes when Rafiki, Simba's teacher, finds the young lion and challenges him to have the courage to take over his leadership role, reclaim Pride Rock, and save the Pride

Lands. We see him developing into a good, strong leader. Simba gets the courage and commitment to go back, driven by his vision of the beautiful, thriving Pride Lands before his uncle took over. He faces up to the terrible moment when his father died, and he returns home—to the source of his pain—to reclaim the land.

Think of how Simba's image of himself changed and how he developed. Think of how he reconnected with his relationships, including with his mother. Think of his vision and his faith. Simba had to stretch and learn and grow into his leadership role before he could assume the mantle—before he could be king.

WHEN GOOD LEADERS MAKE BAD DECISIONS

My Tuck colleague Dr. Sydney Finkelstein has spent much of his career studying mistakes leaders make. He's interested in understanding why their best intentions some-time go awry and how to help them avoid the traps they can stumble into.

In his book *Think Again: Why Good Leaders Make Bad Decisions and How to Keep It from Happening to You* (Harvard Business School Press), Dr. Finkelstein and his coauthors looked at a database of eighty-three decisions through the lens of neuroscience, decision-making theory, and other disciplines to examine the factors that distort a leader's judgment.

"A lot of the failing leaders refused to learn anything new," he says. "It wasn't that they were unable; they were unwilling. They weren't completely unaware of it. Most were people who knew what was going on around them. They had the facts but chose not to cope. That was very common, this unwillingness to learn."

I asked Syd to help us identify the four red flags that put

leaders at risk for making bad decisions. These four ideas can apply to anyone, though I hope not to you. They are a natural aspect of how our brains process information and how we think.

Inappropriate Attachments

People are naturally attached to certain people, places, or things. But sometimes those attachments lead you down the wrong path. "Think of Bernie Madoff," says Dr. Finkelstein. "Some smart, high-level people invested with him because somebody else told them they should. They didn't do the most basic due diligence because they thought they knew him—or knew somebody who knew him."

Inappropriate Self-Interest

Of course everyone is driven by self-interest, which Dr. Finkelstein says is generally unconscious. So without being aware of it, they make decisions that are bad for the organization but good for them. "Self-interest leads to a sense of entitlement," says Dr. Finkelstein. He points to an easy example: the bankers who continued to live large on bonuses and perks even as Wall Street went down in flames. "What's interesting," he adds "is that most of the time if you point out to people that they are acting in a self-interested way, they have no idea what you're talking about, because it's so far below the surface."

Inappropriate Prejudgments

In these cases, someone decides how something is and disregards, ignores, or denies everything else. "This happens a lot," says Dr. Finkelstein. "You look for data to confirm what you want to do and disregard everything else. If there are ten possibilities, but you decide that the only one that will work is number seven, then you don't even consider the other nine. Our most recent former president [George W. Bush] is a classic example of this kind of prejudgment."

Misleading Experiences

Experience should be the best teacher. "But not when you refuse to acknowledge that the world has changed since the last experience you had," says Dr. Finkelstein. For example, in the mid-2000s, bankers made high profits from sub-prime lending. However, the housing and finance markets changed, but bankers across the world continued to take the kinds of risks that led to the collapse of the mortgage market. What worked before now didn't work.

It's sometimes difficult to avoid making a bad decision, especially with so many unconscious factors in play. But when you're faced with a big decision, slow down and consider how the four red flags might be influencing you—and think again.

Leadership: The Essentials

► *Leadership has changed over the past two decades. The old-school, authoritarian father or mother figure who led from the top down is no longer valued. Leadership is now expansive, transparent, and creative.*

► *The best leaders are authentic; they bring their whole selves to work.*

► *The twelve guiding principles of leadership are:*

1. *Self-awareness*
2. *Vision*
3. *Communication*
4. *Results*
5. *Integrity*
6. *Humility*
7. *Teamwork*
8. *Influence*
9. *Commitment*
10. *Passion*
11. *Courage*
12. *Faith*

What's Next?

The next chapter examines work-life balance, a notion that obscures the real challenges for working women. Is it possible to have it all? I will explore the idea of "having it all" and feature real-life high-level women who have managed, with effort, to stay happy and sane.

Chapter 10

Invisible Acts: Work, Life, and Health

ACT I: MORGAN'S PLEA

It is the Friday before Mother's Day. My ten-year-old goddaughter, Morgan, and I are busy at the local Hallmark store in Charlotte, North Carolina, searching for the perfect card for her mom. My cell phone rings. Not thinking, I press the talk button. It's a consulting client calling about an upcoming engagement. Without any hesitation, I move into a conversation with her, signaling to Morgan to continue looking for a card while I do a bit of work.

Morgan's not happy. Her expression is sullen. And the longer I talk, the more irritated she looks. This isn't like her. Morgan is usually warm and kindhearted even when things don't go her way. It takes me a minute or two to realize that our pleasant shopping trip is quickly going downhill.

I finally get it and ask my client if I can call her back on Monday. Shutting off my phone, I ask Morgan, "Are you satisfied now?" And she responds with a very firm yes.

It's not until we're in the car that I am able to ask her what was up in the store. "We used to spend a lot of time together," she says.

"I got to see you almost every day, you helped me with my homework, and we went to get ice cream after school. But now that you live in New Hampshire and teach at Dartmouth, I don't get to see you as much. You spend a lot of time on the road. I miss not having you around. This was supposed to be our time."

As she speaks, tears come to my eyes and I immediately feel guilty. Morgan is right. Between teaching at Tuck, my consulting practice, and speaking engagements, my time in Charlotte has greatly diminished. I love my goddaughter dearly; our relationship is one of the most important ones in my life. Still, I have shortchanged her. On this day I make a promise to Morgan that I will never again take our time together for granted.

ACT II: YOUR FATHER HAS CANCER

I'm traveling across the country, racing from a US Airways flight to catch a Northwest Airlines flight in order to reach still another client. On this particular day I am coming from Los Angeles and heading to Detroit for an evening engagement. Having rushed from the south side of the airport to the north side, I finally settle into my seat exhausted. Before I turn off my cell and stash my bag, the phone rings.

It's my sister Brenda. I start to tell her to call me later. Instead, she says, "Ella, Daddy's test came back today; he has cancer. It's multiple myeloma, advanced stage." The flight attendant signals for me to shut off my phone. But I can't; I am too numb. Here I am sitting among strangers in an airplane about to take off for Detroit, hearing the news that my dad has an advanced stage of cancer.

I say to the fight attendant, "I just found out my dad has cancer." She is compassionate but lets me know that the phone must be turned off now. As the aircraft starts to move, I want to grab my belongings, get off this plane, and find the first jet going to Newark, New Jersey, where my family in crisis waits. As tears run down my cheeks, I know I can't.

ACT III: ASLEEP AT THE WHEEL

It's Mother's Day, and I'm all dressed up. I've just come from church, where I celebrated the mother figures in my life. I've been ripping and running all spring, and I'm ready to slow the hell down, because I'm bone-tired. During the church service, I've become very aware of my fatigue. So I decide to drive home via the local surface streets instead of hopping onto the expressway. I know I'm not alert enough to navigate the highway.

I turn on the radio and tune into the Sunday afternoon jazz show. I'm really getting into the flow of the music as I cruise down the street. Quick as a finger snap, I'm jolted back to reality when my car jumps into the median and into oncoming traffic. When I realize what's happening, I sharply turn the wheel, propelling the car back to my proper lane, but facing the wrong direction. I look up and see cars approaching me head-on; they skid to a stop several feet away from me. I turn my car around and pull off the road to collect my wits. After taking a deep breath, I drive home, go to bed, and fall into a deep sleep that lasts several hours.

ACT IV: CATASTROPHE

It is an early summer, Saturday morning, and I am up with the sun and off to the organic farmer's market in Matthews, a small country village just outside of Charlotte. You can buy the most delicious organic tomatoes there. I head off in my car and by good fortune find a parking space right across the street from my destination. After parking my car, I walk over to the pedestrian crosswalk in the village center, which is one of Matthews's charms.

As I cross, I glimpse, out of the corner of my eye, something large and gray hurtling my way. Calmly, I think to make sure that I'm in the crosswalk, because surely the driver of the vehicle is able to see me. I am a blond-headed black woman in a white Southern rural town—how could he *not* see me? This is the last conscious thought that I am to have for sixteen hours.

The seventeen-year-old young woman who is at the wheel without a license and talking on her cell phone does not see me. The pickup truck she is driving hits me on my left side. Instinctively I must have extended my left hand to meet the force of the oncoming vehicle. The impact of the truck lifts me up in the air, and I land on the concrete face-first.

I don't remember any ambulance sirens or flashing lights, no ER nurses or doctors. I don't recall any of the family and friends who filled the waiting room. What I do remember is looking up at my pastor's face as he is holding my hand. Days later, I will discover that the police sergeant who responded to the accident got the phone number of my best friend and called her. He asked if she knew my minister or priest, who needed to be contacted immediately—along with anyone else who would want to see me—because no one believed I was going to make it through the night.

Through God's grace, I survive with only a compound fracture in my left upper arm, major nerve damage in my left wrist, a serious concussion, a broken nose, five broken teeth, and facial burns. While these injuries seem like an awful lot of damage, I could have been dead or severely impaired for life.

———

These are my four acts. They tell the story of how out of balance my life had become. For me, they represent the neglected imperatives in the lives of working women: Bringing your focus and full attention to the children in your life when they need you. Being available to meet the needs of aging, increasingly frail and vulnerable family members. Feeling burned out, trying to do everything for everyone, including the people you work with, while neglecting yourself. And still finding the grace and stamina to accept those unforeseen catastrophic curve balls that life sends.

All working women face these issues. It's known as work-life balance, and it's one of the hot-button issues in workforce management and a touchstone in the popular press. But that shorthand does nothing to reflect our lives at work and at home and the many, many ways they intersect—and collide.

Creating an ideal work-life balance was the gold standard a decade ago. But in the new corporate reality, and especially for the cream-of-the-crop leadership jobs, that's not enough. Work and life are often one and the same. While many of our mothers and grandmothers worked—and worked hard—the work didn't generally involve global travel, developing informal relationships inside and outside work, attending meetings at all hours, a BlackBerry that's always on, laptops, email, and Facebook.

Work is all-invasive. Work-life balance is not a fifty-fifty deal anymore. You can't stick your work in a box and slam it shut when you're ready to spend more time with your family and friends. In a high-powered position, you'll be working day and night, attending work-related functions, socializing with your colleagues, and traveling across the globe. Work and life are one big mash-up, and you must find a way to manage it as a whole.

I actually find it fascinating, and infuriating, that we are so concerned with the concept of work-life balance. It's a very rational, linear, masculine way to look at the kind of lives that we lead.

The term gives the illusion that you can balance work and the rest of your life. Balance implies that everything is equal. But there is no fifty-fifty. It's your life. You have to look at the whole package and figure out how to make the parts work together—how to build it and shape it so that you, and all the people you love, feel happy, healthy, and fulfilled.

Throughout the book, I've tried hard to remember that my readers include working mothers, some with partners, others without. In this chapter, one of the country's top executives, a single mother, talks about the dramatic wake-up calls that spurred her to retool her life and career—and how she lived to tell about it. Two hard-charging, high-powered execs discuss how they have been able to brave the work-life storm, sometimes uneasily and with great struggle. And finally, another woman, equally accomplished, shares the painful revelation that her job was making her fat and describes how she got her weight under control. I hope my story and theirs inspire you to make sure your own life is in balance, and take the best care of you.

Circus Acts

Circus Acts might feel like a whimsical exercise, but it's actually very illuminating. I've done this exercise with my students, at seminars and workshops, and in companies I consult with.

HOW IT WORKS
You will imagine your life, work, and home as a three-ring circus.

WHAT YOU NEED
Paper

Pens, pencils, or anything else to draw and write with

HOW THIS EXERCISE WILL AFFECT YOUR WORK AND LIFE

It helps you put your life into sharp perspective. Try it and see what you learn about yourself and your life:

Draw three rings—one for work, one for personal life, and one for community involvement. In each ring, draw the circus performer you think represents your role in that sphere. Ringmaster? Lion tamer? Below each of these performers, list your biggest stresses and primary coping mechanisms for each role.

Take a minute and think about that imagery. Do you feel like you're walking on a tightrope with no net underneath, trying to keep everything in balance? Are you barely able to keep the lions at bay? Are you working too hard to make everyone else happy and not looking at what brings you joy? Are your rings unconnected because you feel isolated—you've compartmentalized life from work and can't figure out how to bring it all together?

Now imagine what you'd like the rings to look like. Get a sheet of paper and create an action plan to make it happen. Do you need more help at home? A vacation? A different job assignment? A health care provider for your mother? A new job? Be specific. Then figure out the steps you need to take to get what you need.

You can also build on this circus acts exercise using an exercise below. At the end of this chapter I explain how to create a Picture Prayer, which allows you to imagine a vision of what you'd like your life to look like.

WHEN WORK MEETS LIFE: THE COLLISION

When Michelle Obama became our country's First Lady and First Mom, the issues of work-life balance came into sharp focus. Why is it so hard to have a life? We've been saying throughout this book that you've got to perform, perform, and perform some more. You have to be twice as good. You can't advance unless you have stellar performance and work your tail feathers off. That's code for "You have to be Superwoman." That means taking care of everything and everyone and not showing any vulnerability. Superwoman's mantra? "I can handle it."

It's very hard to go home to family members, partners, and significant others, take off the Superwoman outfit, and hang it up in the closet so that we can become mom, wife, daughter, sister, lover. Too often we race home and move right into the personal dimensions of our lives with the Superwoman outfit still intact. We take charge, dictate, control, and direct. And we aren't taking any prisoners.

When that Superwoman mind-set spills over into personal life, it causes havoc. It tanks our relationships with the people who love us. It causes more distance. It makes us feel more isolated. We have all these emotions and feelings, but they're trapped inside. The little voice inside is telling us we are not doing a good job anywhere—not at work, not at home. The Superwoman persona doesn't allow us to receive the love. So we secretly feel even more vulnerable, even though we're not supposed to tell anybody. Not when everybody keeps saying, "You're so strong."

Work-life balance is really tricky for anyone in this day and age. But it is extremely difficult when we are in Superwoman mode. As you can see from the experiences I shared with you at the beginning of this chapter, the issues of life won't leave you alone. There are moments when personal lives demand all of our attention. If you have a parent with cancer, you've got to be there. If you have children, you have to take care of them. If you have a significant relationship, you have to nurture it. You can't work 24/7 and not expect to fall asleep at the wheel. Sometime, somewhere, you're going to crash.

When It's Time for a Career EKG

Think Debra Sandler and think Splenda. The worldwide president of McNeil Nutritionals, a division of Johnson & Johnson, Debra masterminded the highly successful U.S. launch of the sweetener in the little yellow packets. Her efforts have turned Splenda into the country's number-one sugar substitute. In 2008, she was featured in Black Enterprise *magazine as the corporate executive of the year. Not the corporate* female executive *but the corporate* executive *of the year. Despite all her power and success, Debra admits that twice during her rapid ascent, dramatic events forced her to stop and perform a career EKG. An EKG is a medical procedure that looks at the health of your heart. You need to do the same, says Debra, with your career.*

––––––––––––

When I started as a young pup at PepsiCo as a marketing assistant in the late eighties, I did my first career plan. Success was about getting a promotion to VP. Then I got my first promotion, then the next, and the next. Finally, I was vice president of marketing for a major business and was traveling to Latin America and the Caribbean. I was only thirty-five. I love marketing and I was born and grew up in the Caribbean, so this was a great job. I had a big staff and a substantial budget, and I traveled all the time to a region that was home to me.

But one day I looked up and realized I wasn't fulfilled. Something was missing, lacking. In the short run I wanted to be a marketing VP, and then down the road my dream job was to be chief marketing officer somewhere. But though those goals were on my career plan, I didn't really have a life plan. I had a serious Superwoman complex, and I was burned out. In fact, I was so burned out, I was crispy.

That was just over ten years ago and marked my first career EKG. I got pregnant and my daughter was born in 1997. I was at home on maternity leave and reports of that British nanny case in Massachusetts were all over the news. At the same time, I found out that my company was being spun off. When I returned, I'd have to work harder than ever. So day after day as I watched the reports of the kid's death and the nanny's conviction, I kept thinking, *I have to find a nanny for my daughter, but it doesn't feel right.* My brain said, "Go back into work and prove yourself." But my heart said no. It was extremely difficult, but I never went back. I stepped out of the workforce and became a stay-at-home mom.

Once I arrived at the decision, it was a wonderful release. I spent a great deal of time with my daughter, being a mother, but I also took time to think about what I really wanted to do. I read the books, took the tests, and worked on figuring out what I excelled at and what were the assignments I really liked—and didn't like. I realized that I didn't enjoy an overly structured environment, micromanaging, and cost cutting my way to success. There are people who love this, but I'm not one of them. What I enjoy is freedom, building, creating, and innovating. I like a blank sheet of paper, and I love a job where I can surprise people with the results.

I also decided I wanted to give back. I had spent thirteen years marketing soft drinks and fast food. But at the same time, diabetes is rampant in my family. So many of my relatives have it, had it, or are at risk of getting it. My maternal grandmother, who has been a force in my life, lost both legs due to complications from diabetes. I wanted to do something to make a difference.

After two years at home, I went to Johnson & Johnson. My job was to start up the Nutritionals group and launch Splenda. We rolled out Splenda in 2000, and the following year, I moved to another position in the company. Not long after that, I had my next career EKG.

I was at a meeting in Denver, staying in a wonderful hotel. Sitting in my room, I noticed the room was spinning. I had felt like this a few times during the past couple of months but ignored it. This time the room was spinning but it wouldn't stop. I managed to get up—very elegantly, I think. I made it to the bathroom, then crawled on my hands and knees to the hall, to an area where someone would find me. The next thing I knew, I was in an ambulance.

I thought I had some horrible disease. But it was actually a middle-ear infection, which made me lose my sense of balance. When I asked how I got it, the ER doctor said it was stress-related. He asked me, "On a scale of 1 to 10, how much stress do you have in your life?" I told him I was a 15. That scared me. I was close to forty years old. My father had died on the job; he was rushed to the hospital and three days later he was dead. Getting that infection was a real wake-up call. I had no balance; I couldn't stand up. This was a symbol, a signal that I needed to do something serious to reduce my stress.

I let my boss know I wasn't happy. We agreed that I'd go back to Nutritionals, the division I had left. Going backward doesn't seem like a good career move, but for me it was. This EKG also led to the end of a twenty-year marriage.

It's time for another check-in. This time it'll be a life EKG. There's no baby or ambulance this time, but I'm going to be fifty next year, and I want to take stock. My short-term goal is to look and feel as good as I did at twenty-five.

I know first and foremost that I was put on the earth to give birth to my little girl and to nurture a wonderful woman. And I am also awed by the opportunity to work on developing and marketing products that address pediatric obesity, diabetes, and other metabolic diseases. I'm also clear that I have about ten more years left in corporate America, and there's more I want to do. I want to make sure that whatever I do, it fits my own vision, not someone else's vision of what I should be doing next. The promotions are great; the trappings of the job are wonderful. But if it all went away, I wouldn't change one iota. The most important thing to me is my time—my time with my daughter, my time with my family, and my time with the people who matter to me. I understand that that's what is most precious.

CAN YOU HAVE IT ALL?

I asked two high-octane working mothers this question, and their responses, in the box below, are insightful and illuminating. The short answer is yes, you can have it all, but not at one time. Many career women have learned the hard lesson that they have to pull back from their career aspirations for short or long periods in order to focus on raising children, caring for other relatives, or both. Some women work part-time, flextime, or night shifts, have home-based businesses, consult or freelance from home, or have chosen alternative, less demanding career paths so that they are more available to their families. Others take a break and then return to full-time jobs.

Other working mothers have made different choices. Some

work in more laid-back parts of the country—the South or Midwest instead of New York City. Or they move closer to family and friends who can provide care and support. Others have switched to different family-friendly companies or even industries in order to take back their lives and get some semblance of balance.

The one thing that I know is true is that the modern work-life balancing act takes organization and that proverbial village. I've watched my coauthor on this book keep in touch with a support network for her two children that includes her partner, her mother, her ex, the children's father, and her best friend. (Go ahead and try to figure out that cast of characters!) Via iPhone, emails, and an online bulletin board, she wrangles child care, play dates, soccer practices, tutoring sessions, dentist appointments, family dinners, dance classes, and snow days for her son and daughter as well as her godchildren—all while traveling between New Hampshire, New York, and North Carolina to help me pull together my book. The kids understand that all of their caregivers, even Grandma, have jobs, and that work is important. They also know that they are well cared for and that all of the people in their lives provide a variety of different role models and just love them up.

Being a working mother, single or partnered, also takes flexibility and especially common sense. Might it be better to wait before you go after that big assignment? Sometimes it simply comes down to a game of short-term sacrifices for longer-term gains.

You must also realize that it's okay to ask for and receive help. Sometime it's paid help. Hire a caregiver for your children and get a housekeeper. These are survival tools; there's no shame in needing paid help. Explore the benefits your company offers and take advantage of them.

Keeping all your balls in the air also takes lots and lots of talking. If you're married or partnered, have the hard conversations with your mate. It's rare that a partnership is fifty-fifty. Generally, somebody carries more of the load at home and somebody makes more money. Both might be you. There will be times when it'll be more than 50 percent, other times when it's less. But the bottom line is, do you feel appreciated in what you're doing? When you feel appreciated and loved, don't you stop counting and measuring? It's when you feel unappreciated and unloved that you start calculating who's doing how much.

Discuss your expectations. Do you both want high-rolling careers? Who's supposed to wash the dishes, put the kids to bed, and take out the trash? Can you afford to hire more help? Don't wait until you're at each other's throat to talk things over.

If you're in a relationship, whether married or just dating, keep it fresh. Be creative about spending time together. Don't let the combination of work and family life suck both of you dry. Find ways to connect. Talk to the children, too. Explain what you do and take them to work so that they see for themselves. Let them understand that you love them but that work's important to you, too. Always bring your support team into the conversation, since your life struggles, changes, and decisions affect them as well.

The Career, the Kids, and Everything in Between: A Conversation

I asked two friends, Rosalind Hudnell and Cassandra Walker Pye, to talk about having it all. Between them, these two northern California working mothers have two extremely high-flying careers, two husbands, and seven children. Roz is the chief diversity officer and director of global diversity for Intel Corporation, the world's largest semiconductor manufacturer. By any definition her job is extreme. She has two sons and a daughter. Her husband retired as an executive at

EDS, the global technology company, and now teaches math and coaches high school soccer.

Cassandra, the former deputy chief of staff for California governor Arnold Schwarzenegger, is now senior vice president in the Sacramento office of APCO Worldwide, a global communications consulting firm. She counsels senior executives and political professionals on corporate positioning, market entry, and crisis communication. She and her husband, Kelvin, have four sons, ages thirteen to twenty. Kelvin teaches math and science and returned to school for his bachelor's degree while their children were still in diapers.

––––––––––

Can you have it all?

Roz: You don't want to have it all. It's too hard.

Cassandra: You have to make hard choices. Nobody can have it all, all the time.

Talk about the hard parts.

Roz: Travel. At one point my job took fifty to seventy hours a week, and I was traveling 75 percent of the time globally. My husband, too. One night we were in bed organizing our lives and agreed that we both wouldn't travel out of the same time zone at the same time. My husband also came up with a plan that we would be around on the weekends. Our kids owned us on Friday nights, Saturdays, and Sundays. I could be away between midnight on Sunday until about Friday at 6:00 p.m. I'd take a red-eye out of one time zone on Saturday morning to arrive home by Friday dinnertime. I took an awful lot of red-eyes.

Cassandra: When I first started working for the governor in December 2004, my family suffered, especially my oldest son. I had been a stay-at-home mom, and at other times worked part-time or from home. So this deputy chief of staff job was hard for everyone, including me. I couldn't provide the same kind of structure for the kids, and I really struggled being away from them. I had so little control over my time. I would plan on leaving at 6:00 p.m. to go to a soccer game and then find out at the last minute that I had to be on a plane with the governor. It was hard for me.

Discuss the sacrifices you made for your family.

Roz: We made trade-offs. Cassandra, you might've been on Obama's team. . . .

Cassandra: You might be the head of Intel.

Roz and Cassandra: [Laughing] But we aren't!

Roz: I sacrificed sleep. I also purposely didn't take some assignments that might have been good for my career. I was asked to consider taking the role of technical assistant [a type of chief-of-staff role] to the chairman of the board, but I said no. I'd be dependent on his calendar, his schedule. I have always traveled a lot, but I control my own calendar.

Cassandra: I left my job with the governor. In the summer of 2005, we were all on a family vacation in San Diego, and I got the call that I had to go back two days earlier than planned. We packed up the car and everybody was okay except for me. We stopped to get gas, and my husband and the boys got out to pay while I stayed in the car. The cell phone rang, and it was Maria Shriver, the governor's wife and also a mother to four children. She said she was just calling to check in. I was so angry at that moment that I literally burst into tears. I cried and cried. I told her, "This is the hardest thing I've ever done, and I hate to leave him in the lurch, but I'm done. This is the only six days I've had with my kids this year; I'm done." She told me, "This is about your life and your family. You tell him you will help him to find a replacement and then you leave." And that's what I did.

Roz: I think it's also about what you won't sacrifice and setting family priorities together. My husband and I asked each of our kids to tell us what events were important for them. They helped us make the decisions. My son might say, "Come to this game, because this other one isn't as important." I couldn't go to everything, but I'd prioritize the one thing. I wouldn't miss that game or that event for any reason. Even if the CEO needed me in a meeting on that one day, I wouldn't be there.

It was a commitment I made to my kids, and I have been fortunate that my bosses respected that. But then again, keeping my commitment to my family and my job became part of my brand.

Talk about what you've learned along the way.

Cassandra: I learned that my kids *really* missed me when I was working so much. No one in my family is sad that I don't have that job with the governor. The week I left, my two oldest sons, Richard and William, were out of school for the summer. The three of us flew to Virginia Beach to look at colleges and spend time together. We were at a friend's house and the boys—practically men—were sitting on the couch next to me. They wouldn't move. They were stroking my arms, playing with my ear, constantly touching me. After they went on to something else, my friend asked, "What was that all about?" I told her, "They missed me." I had no idea how much.

Roz: I learned that being a good mother isn't about cooking a four-course meal every night. I used to come home from work and immediately start cooking. One day, when my daughter was five or six years old, she said to me, "Come sit with me and watch TV." I said, "Mommy's got to cook dinner." She said, "I'll eat cereal; I just want you to sit with me." My nine-year-old came downstairs and asked, "What's for dinner?" I said, "Melanie wants me to watch this show, so we're going to have cereal." He said, "Cool." My husband came home and saw what was going on and fixed himself a sandwich. That was an awakening for me, to realize that what my children really wanted from me was my time. Cereal and peanut butter are sometimes good enough.

Describe your support systems.

Cassandra: I was blessed to have a hands-on husband and supportive mother. My mother spent at least six weeks of every summer in California so I could continue to work.

Roz: Me, too, and my grandmother.

Can you have work-life balance in a tough economy?

Cassandra: You may have to go through the fire for a little while. You might have to take a tough assignment that has longer hours and more travel or go back to school to get another degree and leave the kids with your mom for a while.

Roz: And then you can ask. It goes like this: perform, ask, perform, ask. If you are fabulous, you'll get as much work-life balance as you want. But you have to perform and prove yourself. That is the key, and the unpopular thing no one wants to admit. If you deliver results, companies will be more willing to meet your terms to stay.

What mistakes do working mothers make?

Roz: Overexplaining. When building your career, there's a fine line between being transparent about the details of your family life and talking too much. We tend to overexplain the demands of being a working mother. It's better to be clear and say, "I need to leave at this time, but I understand what the deliverable is, and I will get it in on time." Nobody needs to know that you stayed up all night to do it. Keep the details to yourself. It's not that you have to hide who you are, but in the workplace, the thing people care the most about is whether you can get the job done. Honestly, most really don't care what it took you to do it.

Cassandra: I think women don't plan for their families. If you're developing your career but you know that down the line you want to have children, then you need to look at the end game—where you want your career to go and that you want kids. Then work backward to get there. Too many women don't include the children in the career plan. Then they look up and they're over forty and it's too hard and/or too late to start.

Roz: It all goes back to preparation, planning, and performance. If you want to have a baby in four years, you need to start planning now and begin to make yourself indispensable. Then you can leverage that performance to get what you need in the future. You also need to plan how you want to build your career simultaneously with your family. You are one person with many different aspects to your life. When they all work in concert, that is a beautiful thing. But in order to do that, much like a symphony performance, you have to spend time scripting it.

A WORD TO SINGLE WOMEN

Another frustration in the discussion of work-life balance is that it seems to relate only to women with children and/or relationships. This might seem to imply that having a full, balanced life doesn't matter to those of us who are single without children. But it does matter.

If you're single, you've got to make time out to figure out what you want and do the things outside of work that give you joy, depth, and happiness. You deserve that just as much as anyone else.

If you don't have a relationship and you'd like to, first and foremost know one thing that you've definitely heard before: you've got to have a relationship with yourself before you can have one with someone else.

Some of us have pushed ourselves so hard toward work and at work that we've left no room for anyone else or anything else. The places in which we find success are the areas that we continue to develop. It feels good to be successful. So if you're a workaholic, you've gotten affirmation, praise, reward, and visibility from your career. Ten to one, you're going to devote more time to developing it.

On the flip side, if you've gone out on bad dates, had horrific breakups, or think there are no men out there because you've bought into the hype that all the good guys are gone, you're going to continue pushing yourself toward work, where the goodies come from. You won't make the time to develop good relationships, even friendships.

I had an aha moment several years ago. I was working with a group of women and asked them to identify the relationships in their lives using a networking map. In this exercise you create labels—one for yourself and then others for the people closest to you. With yourself in the middle, you build a map using the other labels around you. The first time I did it I had something like fifty significant people. The next time, seven years later, I had only about twelve. And the one closest to me wasn't a person at all. It was Doobie, my fourteen-year-old dog. Here was this poor dog holding on as long as he could so I wouldn't be alone. Professionally, I was on my way. I was at a top-tier school, working on interesting research. But personally, I had become detached from my friends and had no spiritual connections. There were no children on the map, no significant other. I knew right then that I had to get a life.

I ended up leaving that school in two years and went to a less well-known college. I moved out of the Northeastern urban environment, which made me feel isolated, to the South, to a neighborhood where people looked like me. I joined a church and became godmother to some children.

Here's what I love now: spending time with my two goddaughters, who are now fourteen and fifteen years old, and with my godson, Sebenza, who is thirty-one, and his wife, Morrie, and with whom I have developed a wonderful adult bond. Cooking in my gourmet kitchen—when I'm home, I love to hit those pots. I make sure I take a good spa trip to slow everything down and connect with the inner me and ensure I'm watching my health. My girl Belle is my four-legged companion, my road dog. She makes me laugh; she demands that I give her attention—really genuine attention. I've declared Sunday as my higher-calling day. I go to church and sometimes have brunch with my church family. I've also gotten the hang of email and text messaging so I can keep in touch with other friends. I haven't mastered the dating thing yet—and it may be too much for an old girl like me—but at least I understand that companionship is important. I also know that if I want to find a partner, I need to take the time to look, and pursue that goal with as much passion and gusto as I've poured into my career. I just haven't done that yet.

One thing I like to remind single working women of is that sometimes you have to draw the line. People sometimes think that single working women without children can always be there to the pull the weight of every family problem because you have no other responsibilities. Family and friends come to you for help, particularly financial assistance. If you don't say yes, you're labeled as selfish and self-absorbed. Still, you have to learn how to say no when you need to. Each of us has a responsibility to give back, to help family members, to lift as we climb. But don't do it so much and so often that you have little or nothing left for yourself. You deserve a life, too.

Finally, it's also important for everyone, whether you have children and family obligations or not, to be advocates for creating a holistically healthy environment at work. Serve on a work-life task force, organize a workshop, or volunteer for a committee so that everybody's lives are multidimensional.

KEEPING HEALTHY, STAYING SANE

Recently a young woman at a workshop took me aside and haltingly shared how she has been able to manage her extreme job. It took a nervous breakdown to help put her life in balance.

In her mid-thirties, she works for one of the world's largest companies. One of three managers in her division—and in desperate need of several more—she provided services for tens of thousands of employees around the world. Before she was able to rein in her job, she'd roll into the office most days around 6:00 a.m., work all day, and often attend job-related social functions at night. To keep up with the tremendous workload, she also worked many weekends and traveled frequently. Looking back, she realizes that she was stretched way too thin and was both stressed out and burned out. She remembers being in tears almost every day.

A year ago, she lost it. When her manager scolded her about something she'd done wrong, she had an anxiety attack and fell apart. "I freaked out and couldn't stop crying," she says. Totally fried, she checked herself into a hospital and ended up taking a six-week leave of absence. The time she spent away from work gave her a chance not only to recover but also to think.

When she returned to her job, she was determined to find a saner way to work. She had a come-to-Jesus discussion with her manager and persuaded her to hire two more employees. She also took control of her hours and signed up for a class on weekends.

When it came time for her performance review, she assumed that her breakdown had blown any chance of a promotion. But to her shock, her boss didn't agree and promoted her to managing director. "That strengthened my resolve to keep the boundaries in place," she told me. "Corporate America will take everything if you don't hold on to a part of yourself. So I was determined to really hold on to some part of my life."

No matter how busy, important, and powerful you may feel, part of the life plan must be taking care of yourself in every way—physically, emotionally, intellectually, and spiritually. So much is expected of us both at work and at home that we can easily let our bodies go. When everybody else's needs come first, ours come last. We don't monitor our health or pay attention to how we're feeling. We don't go to the doctor; we don't get the checkups and tests we need. We tune out the messages our bodies are trying to send us when something is going wrong. Or we find ways, unhealthy ways, to cope.

Work won't quit; we have to perform and perform some more. So we suck it up until we break down. The breakdown can come in many forms—gaining weight, drinking too much, depression, back problems, migraines, high blood pressure, panic attacks, or, in my case, shopping. Or the breakdown can be a true breakdown.

There are no easy answers. I know that I haven't found any. It's just hard. As the women in this chapter have talked about, it takes courage, determination, and resolve to change. You have to commit to taking good care of yourself and stick to it. Work as hard on yourself as you do on your career. That will mean setting aside time for good health: planning and organizing doctor visits, healthy meals, dental appointments, massages, and trips to the gym; finding a therapist; grabbing some quiet time. Most of us know what we're supposed to do: Eat small, healthy meals throughout the day. Stick to low-fat proteins, fruits, vegetables, and whole grains. Watch the sugar and the alcohol. Do some kind of heart-pounding exercise like walking, biking, running, or just playing hard with kids four or five days a week. Pay attention to your body and your emotions and seek help when you need it. Get enough rest. Find spiritual sustenance through service, prayer, or meditation. Talk about things instead of keeping them bottled up until you explode. Be around people you love and who love you back.

Remember, you can't be good for anybody, whether at work or at home, if you're out of sorts, stressed, unfocused, out of control, hiding and keeping secrets, sick, or depressed. As a leader, you can't ask others to follow you if you're always jumping, turning, hopping, and skipping. You have to slow down long enough and pay attention to help people understand where they're going.

And you're not alone. Hang up the Superwoman cape. Ask for help, and leave yourself open to receiving it. The world that we are in right now demands that we have at least a cup half full rather than an empty cup so that we can continue to make things better.

When the Job Makes You Fat

Pamela El has a job she loves, marketing vice president for State Farm. Two years ago, her company began sponsoring the 50-Million Pound Challenge, and Pam was assigned to travel around the country with Dr. Ian Smith, promoting weight loss and good health.

But her career collided with her own health in 2008 when Pam saw herself in a video about the company's initiative. "I had become the poster child for obesity," she says. "Seeing myself, that big moment, gave me the motivation to change."

———————

When I started the tour in 2007, I was 217 pounds. I was a happy big person. I love my job. I have a great husband. We've been married for fifteen years, and he's my best friend. I have two wonderful stepchildren and other close family. When I started traveling with Dr. Ian Smith, I was at the top of my game professionally. I had high blood pressure and was teetering on diabetes, but basically I thought I was okay.

For the next year and a half I was on the road talking about the effects of obesity, diabetes, high blood pressure, and stroke. Rationally, I knew the facts. But I had never looked in the mirror and applied that to myself. Then I saw myself on that video delivering the message of good health and realized what a hypocrite I was. This wasn't what I wanted. This wasn't my brand. How could I be telling people to be healthy when I wasn't? At that moment I broke down and cried.

That same day, I asked Dr. Ian what I needed to do to change. He said, "Pam, if you're ready, I'll help you change." He's a diet expert, and I'd been traveling with him for over a year and had gained twenty pounds. I could've asked him for help at any time. But I hadn't been ready.

That day I was ready, though. He offered his guidance and gave me his book *The 4-Day Diet*. I won't lie: losing weight is one of the hardest things I've ever done. But it's also one of the most important things I've done.

In life just about everything is gray. But weight loss is black and white: calories in, calories out. I had learned how to put excuses on the table to make this black-and-white proposition gray. "I'm on the road, and it's hard to find healthy food. I have to work late, but the gym closes at ten." I had to say to myself, "Yes, I travel a lot; yes, I work hard. But I'm going to lose weight." I had to learn to put weight loss first.

It's also about preparation and planning. I had to schedule time to go to the gym and stick to it. I had to get up earlier before a flight to throw some grapes, an apple, and a snack bar into my bag rather than eat the fast food at the airport. I had to be prepared and determined.

I'm now seventy pounds lighter and I've gone from a size eighteen to an eight. I have cut my high blood pressure medicine in half, and my doctor says that soon I'll be able to come off it altogether. I have absolutely walked away from diabetes. What's been the best part for me is how much my appearance has motivated other people. I've had hundreds of people tell me that my story inspired them. Having this physical transformation allows other people to look at me and say, "If she can do it, I can do it." That's very gratifying to me.

Creating the Life You Want in Pictures

As I close out this chapter, I'd like you to do a last exercise, the Picture Prayer. It allows you to visualize the life you'd like.

I don't remember the first time I heard about a Picture Prayer or who told me about it. I wish I did know, because I'd love to thank that person for passing on such a precious gift to me. I remember the first time I made one; it was over twenty-five years ago. It was at the end of the fall semester of my second year of graduate school at Case Western Reserve. I was struggling to find financing for my third year in the doctoral program. Graduate school was more than a bit challenging; it was downright daunting. I was trying to figure out how I could survive. I didn't want to start off a new year under these circumstances.

It was about this time that someone told me to make a Picture Prayer.

HOW IT WORKS

Think about the kinds of relationships, people, activities, and things you'd like to have in your life—at work, at home, in your community. On a piece of paper, create a collage using pictures and symbols cut out of magazines or downloaded from your computer, then write an affirmation under each picture. Hang your prayer on a wall where you can look at it every day and say the affirmations you have written. Simple!

WHAT YOU NEED

Supplies

Friends

Food

A free afternoon to dream about what you'd like to bring to your life and create that vision

When you think about getting a life, it may be time to create a prayer in pictures.

I took the idea one step further. I went to a crafts store and brought brightly colored construction and tissue paper, glitter, and colored markers. I invited several of my good sister friends over for a Sunday afternoon Picture Prayer potluck. I asked them to bring a favorite dish and also a cherished poem. Everyone was intrigued with the idea.

We began our Sunday afternoon sitting in a circle on the floor. One by one, we took turns reading our poems. Then we meditated on what we wanted to attract into our lives. What were our dreams? What kind of person or people did we want to share our lives with? What would bring us joy in the coming year? What was missing in our lives? After the mediation we made a list of those things that came to our minds.

With some good music playing in the background, we began our collages. One friend planted herself on my bed in the bedroom. Another worked in the kitchen. Several stayed in the living room, while others picked different corners in the dining room. Every now and then someone would call out for a particular kind of picture, like a cart of flowers, an airplane, or a pair of sneakers.

I focused on my needs for school. A wonderful woman named Mary Joyce Green had told me about the Minority Fellowship Program offered by the American Sociological Association (ASA). While my area of studies was organizational behavior, not sociology, the ASA was open as long as your area of study involved some aspect of minority life, which mine did. So on my Picture Prayer I put a photocopy of the application for the fellowship that I had recently completed. My affirmation was short: "God help me find a way to pay for school."

An hour later, we gathered back in our circle to look at our sacred work. Each Picture Prayer looked like a work of art. They were beautiful. One by one, we explained the meanings of our prayers in pictures. My friend who called out for the picture of a cart of flowers wanted to start a garden in her yard. The one who added an airplane dreamed of traveling to Italy. My girlfriend with the picture of sneakers wanted to go to the gym on a regular basis. And on and on the circle went. We listened intently and lovingly. It wasn't so much that we wanted major changes in our lives; rather, we wanted simple things that would make each day a little bit sweeter. When everyone was finished, a friend who was attending divinity school said a closing prayer. We ate wonderful food and talked in great expectation.

Gradually the reports came in. We each received a postcard from Trish as a token of her trip to Italy. Joanette invited us to her garden for tea. Another friend lost weight. As for me, I received a letter from the American Sociological Association congratulating me on my scholarship. I was an ASA Minority Fellow, with funding for the next three years of schooling.

Over the years my Picture Prayers have changed. I have moved away from placing pictures of material things and have started to use images that relate to my spiritual needs. I now create peaceful and spiritual images to remind me to deepen my faith and connection to God. My Picture Prayers are full and colorful, but when my life is complex and hectic, I deliberately make my Picture Prayer simple. It is a reminder for me to slow down. There are pictures of my godchildren and my students. Of course, there is Belle, my Jack Russell terrier, with me at the beach. There are books, because I love to read and write. It is a centering and loving process.

Invisible Acts: The Essentials

► *Creating a perfect work-life balance used to be the gold standard. But in the new, more complex corporate landscape, that's not enough. Work and life have become so entwined that you must find a way to manage them not separately but as a whole.*

► *Can you have at it all? Yes, but probably not all at once. Like many other women, particularly working mothers, you'll need to figure out your own way to make it all work together.*

► *If you're in a relationship—partnered or dating—find ways to connect with your loved one. Talk to family members, children included, about what your job and career mean to you. Be honest about what you're going through, and ask for help if necessary. If you're single, be vigilant about finding ways to stay connected to other people.*

► *You can't advance unless you work, produce, and show results. But you also must pay attention to your own needs and health—physical, emotional, and spiritual.*

► *Remember that you can have the life that you want and deserve—including a thriving, satisfying career.*

IT'S YOUR TIME

Thank you for your time and attention. I sincerely hope you've seen yourself in this book and that, like a GPS, it's helped you as you navigate your own career terrain. I am excited for you and for all that's ahead. It's a good time; it's your time. The door has been kicked wide open, and there's a place for you at the table. In fact, there has never been a better time and more opportunity for women in the corporate marketplace. You might have to pull up a chair—or even bring your own—but the place setting is there. It's up to you to claim it.

Even as I write this, the economic crisis looms large and long. It demands a complete transformation of corporations worldwide. Companies and entire industries throughout the country and around the world must reinvent themselves or die.

You may be feeling the pressure and the pain, but know that companies need us more than ever. Corporations are on the lookout for new, fresh, diverse talent to reimagine and guide a new global economy. When this economic crisis ends, they will be looking even harder.

The fact is, it's a numbers game. Within the next three or four years, women and people of color will make up 83 percent of the incoming international workforce; globally, white men will constitute only 3 percent. Europe is already having trouble matching qualified people with open positions. In the United States, for the first time ever, women are poised to become the majority of the workforce.

We are the leaders of tomorrow . . . and today. Leadership comes naturally to women. We are flexible, organized, and great at juggling; multitasking is our mantra. We work well with others and know how to manage up and down. If there's something we don't know, we're not afraid to ask about it, listen, and learn.

Now is the time to make opportunities happen. Now is the time to create a new vision of yourself as a professional and a woman. Now is the right time for you to walk into positions of authority, leadership, and power. And as you move into these leadership positions, now is the time to bring your whole, authentic self to the table—and that includes the spiritual, psychological, emotional, and personal.

I hope this book has helped you to prepare, because I truly believe that it's your time!

Please keep in touch and reach out if you have questions, concerns, or stories to share. At ASCENT—Leading Multicultural Women to the Top, the organization I founded several years ago, we will continue to guide you as you actualize your dream as a leader at your companies and in the communities where you live. Please visit our website, ascentleadership.org. Think of it as your coach, your ally, your advocate, and a place to find information and advice and make connections with women like you.

Afterword

Memorandum to the Executive Team

TOPIC: STORM WARNING—ARE YOU PAYING ATTENTION?

Yes, this country is trapped in the worst economic recession since the Great Depression. The nation's banks, once respected, have faltered, requiring massive federal bailouts to survive. Wall Street is a wreck as stock prices rise and fall like a roller coaster. Detroit's Big Three automobile companies, which led the industrial revolution, are fighting for survival. Economic anxiety is high as Americans from all walks of life are being forced to redefine the American dream as they confront home foreclosures. And massive layoffs are occurring across all industries. Yes, times are really bad.

But there is another storm brewing out there in the not-so-distant future. This storm isn't going to hit hard all at once; this is a slow-moving storm that will fully reach its peak in twenty years. But it is a storm that needs close monitoring. Now is the time to start paying attention. This storm isn't going to cause people to be laid off. It will not create a shake-up in any one industry, but its impact will be brutal and include all industries.

What kind of storm is it? It's a storm that is already redefining your workforce. If you are not paying attention, this storm will create huge gaps in your succession plans. This storm is going to trump your ability to hire the best and brightest talent. This storm is going to take away your ability to sell your products not only here in the United States but everywhere else in the world as well. And most people still aren't paying attention to the weather forecasts.

The forecast is right before your eyes. In fact, you even know certain facts about this storm:

- Only 28.6 of all executive managers in the U.S. are women.[*]
- Only 7.4 percent of the all first-level managers are women.[†]
- Between 2006 and 2016, 68.3 percent of the entrants into the U.S. labor force will be women or people of color.[‡]
- Only 3.2 percent of U.S. corporate officers are women of color.[§]
- By 2050, 54 percent of the U.S. population will be people of color; translate this statistic into potential purchasing power.[¶]

Yes, there is a storm brewing. The person you pass the company baton to may not be Jack, Hugh, Bob, or Richard. It may well be Carla, Nancy, Maria, or Kusum, but only if you have prepared for the changing weather. From all current indications, too many corporations still have a very long way to go to get their houses in order.

Too many of you are still looking for that one woman star to bring into the company's executive ranks. Extra points are given if that star also happens to be a woman of color. Your approach is framed as "talent acquisition," even when you have talented

---

[*] EEOC 2007.

[†] EEOC 2007.

[‡] Mitra Toosi, Bureau of Labor Statistics, "Employment Outlook: 2006–2016—Labor Force Projections to 2016: More Workers in Their Golden Years," Monthly Labor Review (November 2007).

[§] Catalyst Census of Women Board Directors, 2008.

[¶] Population Projection, released Thursday, August 14, 2008, U.S. Census Bureau.

and skilled women among your company's ranks just waiting for a chance. But you prefer to send them a message that you are not serious about their advancement. You leave them feeling that they are not competent enough, that they're unworthy of leadership roles, or that you simply aren't interested.

What's worst? Perhaps you have taken the time or made the commitment to develop your female employees and managers. But you continue to mismanage them by not giving them constructive feedback and not providing the mentoring, sponsorship, and critical assignments they need to develop their managerial muscle. Rather than being proactive in their advancement and retention, you have made the explicit choice to close the door while you engage in a star search. Too many women are left sitting in their offices, wasting their time and yours.

Start paying attention to your succession plans. You'd better have multicultural women in your company's pipeline because they are going to be your company's backbone. Where are your women in these plans? Do you have women of color represented in your succession plan? What is the SAR (succession, advancement, and retention) score for all women represented in your company? Where are the women of color on your board of directors? It is time to start paying attention.

Another strong storm indicator is the discrepancy between men's and women's compensation, also known as pay equity. Early in 2009, President Obama signed the Lilly Ledbetter Fair Pay Act, designed to reduce wage inequalities between the genders. Not long after, the *New York Times* reported that "female managers of production workers earn nearly 30 percent less than their managers," while women executives earn less because "too many lead nonprofit organizations where the pay is lower."

While there is no one study that explains why pay inequalities continue to exist, it is time to make this situation right. It's really very simple: women must receive equal pay for equal work just like the men. Are you paying attention?

At the eye of the storm is an issue that will only fester as the number of women continues to climb above 50 percent in the workforce: work-life balance. During the current economic turmoil, the work-life balance discussion has been moved to the back burner. But sooner or later it will return as a front-burner matter, and you'd better be paying attention. Understand that this is not a matter that concerns only women with children or only women. Instead, work-life balance, in one way or another, impacts all employees, even the single ones, even men. Technology only serves to heighten the problem. With technology, work invades every aspect of our lives 24/7. Work-life balance is an issue that cuts across every industry, every sector, and every rank. Antiquated ways of thinking about it will not work. Your company must find the answers to hard questions prior to designing policies and programs. Those of you in the E suite and C suite must ask: "What does competence look like in this company? What are the most effective and efficient ways to engage the work? How can the work be redesigned?"

On the other hand, navigating through this storm may require bigger and bolder approaches. For example, a presidential commission consisting of scholars, executives, practitioners, and diverse men and women across ranks, industries, and sectors could use their knowledge and wisdom to develop a set of national guidelines for addressing work-life balance in this country. My idea may read like pie in the sky to you, but we do need some heavyweight thinkers and everyday people to combine forces and help us untangle the complexities of meshing one's work with the rest of one's life.

This matter becomes more urgent every day as our workforce becomes more female. Where does your company stand?

There is a storm coming. It will change the face of the American workforce. Unlike other storms, this one can have a positive outcome. If you prepare for this storm now, it will usher in an era of the advancement and placement of the most talented, most well-prepared, and most capable women into the highest ranks of companies throughout the world. It will signal the continual growth of women assuming positions in managerial ranks and on all levels throughout your company. Are you ready?

In Gratitude

Behind every book is a story. The genesis of *Career GPS* came as a result of writing the column "Working It" for *Essence* magazine. It offered career advice geared toward African-American women, yet it found its ways into the hands of women from all racial and ethnic groups, representing all industries and professions. Their inquiries challenged me to find a route to offer a more comprehensive way to discuss issues related to women's careers and the changing world of work. After writing *Our Separate Ways: Black and White Women and the Struggle for Professional Identity*, coauthored with Dr. Stella Nkomo, I swore off writing any more books. That book took us ten years to research and write, a painful and grueling process. In *Our Separate Ways*, we illuminated and differentiated the obstacles black and white women experienced in the workplace. Now, I felt compelled to share what I knew about women succeeding in the global corporate marketplace.

This book was conceived and written with the support and encouragement of many people. I am deeply grateful to my editor Dawn Davis, Maya Ziv, and everyone at HarperCollins. Thank you so much for all your good, hard work. My heartfelt thanks to Barbara Lowenstein and Madeleine Morel, my literary agents, for their belief and commitment to my work and to me. When I was willing to walk away from this project for all the wrong reasons, theirs was the voice of reason. I am so thankful that I listened to both of you. They also reconnected me to Linda Villarosa, a brilliant writer, my coauthor.

As it turned out, Linda was my senior editor at *Essence*. We knew each other but had never developed a relationship. During our writing of *Career GPS*, I developed a deep respect for Linda, and for the knowledge, energy, and wisdom she brought to our collaboration. Thank you, Linda, for understanding my vision, for hearing my voice and honoring it.

Writing this book represents only one part of my life. The Tuck School of Business, where I serve on the faculty, is another important component. To my dean, Paul Danos, and the senior associate dean, Robert Hansen, thank you so very much for creating the fertile ground to write this book. In a school that has tremendous commitment to scholars and scholarship, I appreciate your understanding for my need to address everyday issues and touch the lives of women and men beyond the walls of academia. Patricia Hunt, my assistant, did a great job managing my schedule, getting Linda wherever I needed her to be, and just making it through the past year. What would I do without you? To my Leadership Out of the Box students, who teach me so much, I am indebted to the patience and understanding you had while I was writing this book. Your commitment, vision, and drive for making a difference in the world deeply touch me.

Thank you so much to all of the women (and men) who contributed their personal stories, experience, and expertise to these pages. It is your willingness to share your truths and knowledge that deepen this book and make it come alive.

Not too long ago, I created a not-for-profit organization—ASCENT—Leading Multicultural Women to the Top. Our goal is the retention and advancement of professional, multicultural women in corporate America, through executive education, corporate partnerships, and thought leadership. To our corporate partners: PepsiCo, Intel, the American Express Company, MTV Networks, and DiversityInc., thank you for all your support and your commitment to multicultural women. To my board of directors: I appreciate all your encouragement and for giving me the space to create this book. Many of the exercises described in this book are part of ASCENT's curriculum. I am indebted to ASCENT's skillful instructors and coaches, who willingly share their wisdom and gifts with ASCENT's fellows. Their knowledge and insights enhanced my wisdom about leadership and women and their careers. Special thanks go to Michael Chapman, who served as our first executive director, and Carolyn Henderson, the director of coaches. I would be much remiss not to mention our ASCENT fellows, a great group of women we have had the privilege to work with. Each woman has so clearly demonstrated that she belongs at the leadership table. Thank you for confirming what I already knew: if given the development and opportunity, women from all backgrounds can use their voices to make the corporate world a better workplace for both women and men. I am also deeply indebted to the folks at Case Western Reserve University, particularly my advisor, Donald M. Wolfe, who guided my thinking on the many exercises that appear in this book. Don's work on adult education and experiential learning has been invaluable, and I am grateful for the knowledge, wisdom, and generous spirit he shared with me.

This book would not have been written without the encouragement and support from my loved ones. Stella, while we didn't write this book together, you were my sounding board and my confidant. Who else but you would take my calls late at night in South Africa to listen to the next chapter or to help me refine an idea? Our friendship has meant so much to me; you have been such a blessing in my life. To my godchildren, Morgan, Sebenza, Morrie, and Bria . . . life is so much sweeter with all of you in my life. And thank you to my family and friends for understanding my disappearing act while I was writing this book. I can't leave out my four-footed one, Belle—the one creature who demanded I make time for her, provided me with much-needed laughter, and gave me a very important gift throughout the writing process: unconditional love.

Index

About the Authors

ELLA L. J. EDMONDSON BELL, PH.D., is the founder and president of ASCENT—Leading Multicultural Women to the Top, as well as an associate professor of business administration, Tuck School of Business at Dartmouth University. Dr. Bell is also the coauthor of the groundbreaking and critically acclaimed book *Our Separate Ways: Black and White Women and the Struggle for Professional Identity* (Harvard Business School Press). She has written several articles for *Essence* magazine and wrote the monthly "Working It" column. Frequently quoted by journalists, Dr. Bell has been featured in the *Wall Street Journal, BusinessWeek, Newsweek, Working Mother,* and *Fast Company,* among many other business and general audience publications. She lives in Hanover, New Hampshire, and Charlotte, North Carolina.

LINDA VILLAROSA is a former editor at both *Essence* magazine and the *New York Times,* where she wrote or edited a number of award-winning articles. She is the author of several books, including the bestseller *Body & Soul: The Black Women's Guide to Physical Health and Emotional Well-Being.* Her first novel, *Passing for Black,* was published in 2008. Villarosa teaches media studies and writing at the City College of New York and lives in Brooklyn.